O'Neil Ford Duograph 1: Chilé

House at Punta Pite, 2003-06

Smiljan Radic

Crypt in the Cathedral of Santiago de Chilé, 1999-2006

Rodrigo Pérez de Arce

O'Neil Ford Duograph Series, Volume 1
Chile - House, Crypt
The University of Texas at Austin
Center for American Art and Design and
O'Neil Ford Chair in Architecture

Editors
Kevin Alter
Wilfried Wang

Essays
Kevin Alter
Smiljan Radic
Rodrigo Pérez de Arce
Wilfried Wang

Photographs
Kevin Alter
Sebastián Bianchi
Patricio Mardones
Cristobal Palma

Series Editors
Kevin Alter
Michael Benedikt
Barbara Hoidn
Wilfried Wang

Production Editor
Christine Wong

Design by
Matthew Slusarek

Cover Photographs
Christobal Palma

O'Neil Ford duograph 1--Chile : house at Punta Pite, 2003-06, Smiljan Radic : crypt in the Cathedral of Santiago de Chile, 1999-2006, Rodrigo Perez de Arce / editors, Kevin Alter, Wilfried Wang ; essays, Smiljan Radic ... [et al.] ; photographs, Kevin Alter ... [et al.]. -- 1st ed.
p. cm. -- (O'Neil Ford duograph series ; v. 1)
ISBN 978-3-8030-0685-1
1. Architecture--Chile--21st century. 2. Radic, Smiljan, 1965---Criticism and interpretation. 3. PÈrez de Arce, Rodrigo--Criticism and interpretation. I. Alter, Kevin. II. Wang, Wilfried. III. Radic, Smiljan, 1965- IV. Title: O'Neil Ford duograph one--Chile. V. Title: House at Punta Pite, 2003-06, Smiljan Radic. VI. Title: Crypt in the Cathedral of Santiago de Chile, 1999-2006, Rodrigo Perez de Arce. VII. Series.
NA865.6.O54 2008
720.983--dc22
2008013270

Printed and bound in Canada

Sole Distributor in Europe:
Ernst Wasmuth Verlag SmbH & Co.
D-72072 Tübingen, Germany
www.wasmuth-verlag.de
info@wasmuth-verlag.de

ISBN 978-3-8030-0685-1

Sole Distributor in the United States of America and Canada:
D.A.P./Distributed Art Publishers
155 Sixth Avenue, 2nd Floor,
New York, N.Y. 10013, U.S.A.
Tel. (212) 627-1999, Fax. (212) 627-9484

Contents

O'NFD 1

Foreword

On Richness and Depth

Kevin Alter & Wilfried Wang

The *O'Neil Ford Duograph* series intends to provide a platform for significant contributions to contemporary architecture through the collaborative efforts of the Center for American Architecture and Design (CAAD) and the O'Neil Ford Chair in Architecture at The University of Texas at Austin. Each duograph issue will present in detail one building by two different architects from a single country. Descriptions from the respective architects and external critics will complement these building studies. Parallel to the *O'Neil Ford Duographs* will be a sister series entitled the *O'Neil Ford Monographs*, also produced by the Center for American Architecture and Design and the O'Neil Ford Chair. This latter series will document the complex gestation of single buildings of central importance to architecture.

We mark the beginning of the new duograph series with two built interventions from Chilé: a house on the coast in Papudo by Smiljan Radic and the crypt of the Cathedral of Santiago de Chilé (almost two hours from Papudo) by Rodrigo Pérez de Arce. The series editors wish to thank both Smiljan Radic and Rodrigo Pérez de Arce, and of course their numerous collaborators, for having accepted our invitation to form the first pair of architects to be presented in this format. Both architects practice in the capital of Chilé; both lead small offices; both have known each other for years and have been teachers at the School of Architecture at the Pontifical Catholic University of Chilé. Despite the decades of political turmoil and economic instability surrounding the school, under the long serving Dean Fernando Oyarzun, it has been a leader in the South American and international architectural discourse.

Whereas the northern hemisphere has oft neglected the southern hemisphere in cultural as well as other matters, the curious and open minded, critical, and sensitive observers in Santiago de Chilé have evidenced their breadth of awareness of contemporary architecture in numerous and impressive publications, most notably in the journal *ARQ* and its related monographs.

As areas within the post-industrialized northern hemisphere revalue the rate of new construction seen in the context of global climate change, conditions in the northern hemisphere will paradoxically begin to resemble those of the advancing economies in the South. Without wishing each building to be reduced to a polemic against the sated post-industrialized societies, it is a fair assertion that decades of need and externally enforced constraints have increased the intellectual and creative agility of a generation of architects in the southern hemisphere. The ingenuity and resourcefulness achieved in some of the most significant buildings seen in South America will serve as powerful paradigms to the North.

The Center for American Architecture and Design and the O'Neil Ford Chair in Architecture at The University of Texas at Austin are aware of their unique situation: located in the far south of the USA, Austin is an ideal port of call for visitors from South America. While not only architectural models but also ideologies have been exported from the USA to the South – unfortunately, mostly not to the long-term benefit of the South – at the beginning of the 21st century, it is patently clear that much stands to be gained by the northern territories from paying attention to the recent architectural achievements in South America.

Both the *O'Neil Ford Duograph* and *Monograph* series are pointed in their organization. In contrast to mainstream architectural publishing's general inclination to present buildings through a limited collection of canonical images and drawings, these book series strive to show the richness that is inherent in select outstanding architectural works, beyond what is easily consumable. To this end, we present each building through multiple images and drawings with the richness and detail that their complexity demands – thereby both representing them appropriately and exposing them as a counter-argument against the all too common understanding of buildings that are superficial in their meaning and value.

Buildings do not travel well, and images and drawings are a poor substitute for their bodily experience. However, the many perspectives presented here demonstrate something of the deep richness inherent in these works through images that capture the complex nature of a place arising from the vicissitudes of light and weather, of detail and physical/material quality, of view and prospect, and of the patina of use and making. Through this wealth of information, we invite the reader to make comparisons and to enter into these buildings through a deeper vision of their character, through photographs that explain the relationship of circumstance and those that describe the material qualities of stone, concrete, glass, and wood, and through moving back and forth between drawings that describe organization and those that describe detail.

We put these publications forth with the hope that they might be understood both as a means of exposing extraordinary works of architecture to a broader audience, as well as an argument to understand and appreciate buildings through their deep, unmitigated complexity and depth. Short of visiting the buildings oneself in the company of their architects, these duographs will offer as comprehensive, as intimate, and as immediate a contact with the buildings as possible.

We believe that the broad and in-depth presentation of two buildings in one publication is a realistic way by which the printed medium can retain its character when seen in relation to other media. The knowledge embedded in the traditional collection of bound pages, its constant and immediate availability regardless of the proximity of an electric socket and access to the internet, the ease of turning back and forth from drawing to photograph, the idea of a series of publications gracing the shelves — all these reasons refresh bibliophilic faith in an age of the World Wide Web. The printed book did not bring about the death of architecture; the World Wide Web will not kill the book. Instead, we seek to benefit from every medium as it adapts to the presence of the others.

Corporeal Architecture

Kevin Alter, Wilfried Wang

On the face of it, Smiljan Radic's House at Punta Pita and Rodrigo Perez de Arce's crypt of the Cathedral of Santiago de Chile are two commissions that could not be further apart from each other: the one affirming the realm of the living, the other dedicated to the dead.

As opposite as they might seem, the conceptual framework and design constraints that each building confronts define the temporal and spatial limits of architecture themselves. Each project is a fundamental instance of architecture's need to constantly reestablish its temporal presence with every act of building. Depicted here are the first and the last house, as it were: the one on the coastal paradise built for the financially independent "Adam" and the other right at the colonial heart of the city that bears the name of the biblical St. James, name giver to numerous cities in the Spanish speaking world (notably Santiago de Compostela in Spanish Galicia).

Both built interventions are of course forms of colonialization. Where prior cultures existed, the introduction of Christian religion and European ethics set these two buildings in the longer synchronic context, while also representing the more immediate form of colonialization of domestic life in the countryside. The privileged sites – the spectacular Pacific coast and the heart of the Catholic seat in Chilé – each demand from the architects a built statement regarding not only a subjective take on architecture's significance but also, more generally and of wider significance, an objective proof of architecture's role and power to communicate shared values.

In searching for the most concentrated form of the house of the living or the house of the dead, each architect is seeking to connect the specific design to its roots: the primitive hut and the tomb; Adam's house in paradise and man's anti-chamber to heaven; and paradise and heaven as utopias. Each architecture therefore seeks to reconnect to the credible foundations of architecture in general. How does contemporary architecture establish this credibility? Which spatial and formal elements, which materials and details, and which atmospheres are able to reconnect the user to the roots of understanding and credibility that architecture has always possessed?

Given the two utopias – paradise and heaven – the onus on architecture is the greater. In their separate ways, Smiljan Radic and Rodrigo Perez de Arce have provided their answers to the above questions. The memories of paradise and heaven, regardless of the foundations of profane or sacred belief – call upon a specific approach or attitude that could be circumscribed as an architecture of corporeality. Such an architecture can stand both for itself as well as for a given purpose. An architecture of corporeality is concerned with real presences, immediate materiality, palpable physicality.

Meaning in architecture is often understood as it is defined through some sort of translation, through legible reference, and often through metaphorical reading. However, architecture exists, despite the words that are written about it, and the values that an architecture of corporeality communicates are strikingly self-evident. Such an architecture states its specific conception without mediation. A dogged realism of tangible elements, of actual matter, and direct connections to the conditions of circumstance characterize the experience of this architecture and are the locus of its meaning.

Here, abstraction is paramount as a tool, not as a language. It is utilized to emphasize the physical qualities of a place, as a datum against which the exigencies of circumstance are measured, and as a device to confront the user with a direct experience of these qualities. The result is a powerful architecture that exposes what has lain unquestioned. It presents material fact as it is, in the forefront of the users' experience, and consequently encourages them to reflect on its relative meaning.

While the circumstance and materiality that define both of these buildings are powerfully present in their experience, the buildings are hardly innocent bystanders in stewardship of these characteristics. In an architecture of corpo-reality, form is unambiguously forthright, but it is also not the primary source of meaning. Specific aspects of place are brought forward; others are suppressed. Here the house of the living and the house of the dead confront their visitors with a rich and more powerfully present perspective on the conditions of their respective circumstance. They give one pause, promote reflection and encourage the visitor to see the world afresh.

E. 9900
E. 9950
E. 10000
E. 10050
N. 10150
N. 10100
N. 10050
N. 10000
0 1 2 3 4 5 10 20

House at Punta Pite, 2003-06

Smiljan Radic

On the Edge

Kevin Alter, Wilfried Wang

The sun and the sea — with any mention of them, images and memories instantly surface. Who can resist their appeal? Maritime sojourns have been a pastime of Western civilization for centuries. Whether at the villas of Italy of the 18th century, the pleasure gardens of England of the 19th century, or the continuous strip development of the 20th-century Spanish Mediterranean waterfront, appreciative individuals and entire families have made their way to the edges of continents to secure accommodations from which to enjoy the refreshing climate, a view of the sea, and physical contact with the water itself.

The maritime lure has brought about similar developments along the 4000 miles of Chilé's seemingly unending coastline, a striking aspect of the country's geographic and geometric character. Apart from established resorts such as Viña del Mar, La Serena, or Bahía Inglesa, there is increasing development of freestanding houses and condominiums along the waterfront. In the rush to the edge, there are few signs of building control or development sensitivity. It is probably only a matter of time until the same fate of North America and Southern Europe befalls the Chilean coastline. Given this imminent threat, one almost feels grateful to the wealthy property owners who purchase large stretches of coastal property for their individual houses — at least in this way, some semblance of nature is preserved. Even though the act of building right next to the water ensures the property owner as direct as possible a relation to it, the potential presence of neighboring houses inevitably upsets the sense of a privileged privacy. An exclusive relation between onlooker and the sea is the unspoken ideal, as it alone generates infinite awe. This sense of awe has inspired generations of onlookers, be they artists or poets, holiday-makers or property owners. But it is also a sense that puts the onlooker in an ambiguous stance to the vast sea: onlooking from a safe vantage point, from a point of control, while simultaneously fearing the unfathomable embrace of the ocean.

The site for Smiljan Radic's house is an exclusive one, and it has an additional quality: on the southern side is a narrow promontory, while to the distant north is a mountain ridge. Together these elements create a grand bay into which the head of the main volume of the house faces. Most importantly, there is no other visible sign of inhabitation from this property: it is a privileged location indeed, a perfect setting for primal communion with nature.

Our haptic and imaginative relationship with the sea, perhaps best encapsulated by J.M.W. Turner's convulsively romantic seascapes or by the reflective subliminal painting *The Monk by the Sea* (1809-10) by Caspar David Friedrich, is indicative of the ambiguous sense that an individual might have with nature's largest body. Today the architect's task could be to simply gloss over these ambiguities with an infinitesimal promontory to provide a bunker-like shelter or an aloof luxurious retreat. Radic's residential complex resists this safe, unconscious act of building. In their siting, configurations, and choice of materials, the components of the Punta Pite house – the main volume, the pool, and the children's house – each explore different degrees of empathy with the topography.

Traveling along the coastal highway, one observes how the landscape drops precipitously to the sea and could easily miss the drive down to the Punta Pite house in the presence of the ubiquitous views to the ocean and coastal escarpment. Relatively arid with low lying vegetation, local features of the landscape give way, as the sinuous line of the rocky coast and the expanse of the Pacific Ocean capture the visitor's attention. One descends steeply upon entry, traversing the site at an angle to ease the slope for driving, until arriving at a small plaza precariously situated on the edge. Two

Adolphe Appia, Espace Rhythmique: "Die Zypresse," ("The Cypress") 1909, (Inv. no. IV 750 (F409)), 43.6cm x 49.7cm, Deutsches Theatermuseum, Munich

3-meter high, cast-in-place concrete walls and rough concrete pavers mark a crisp edge to the sea. This is the roof of the main building, which is both the extended ground plane of the rocky slope and a plinth on which a collection of stone monoliths are arrayed, almost casually.

Like Adolphe Appia's Espace Rhythmique (1910/11) the few architectural elements are mere frames against which a shadow may fall and a view is presented. Some of the stones stand tall, while others lay on the ground, seemingly resting or knocked over by some terrible storm long past. Like a marker of some previous culture, they seem purposeful, yet without obvious explanation. They appear constructed, shaped, yet without any clear indication of how or why; their marks and scars suggest the story of how they came to be. They seem a palimpsest for the events that have taken place here or elsewhere, and their serendipity is a harbinger of the experience of the house. These objects by the sculptor Marcela Correa populate a stage-like terrace, a still-life of eleven basalts, ambiguously mediating between Rapa Nui heads, abstracted figures, and archaic pillars and beams. Other associations arise: Giorgio de Chirico's *The Enigma of the Oracle* (1910), in which a shrouded figure to the extreme left of the frame overlooks an unbound terrace towards a coastal village. The

Giorgio de Chirico, The Enigma of the Oracle, 1910 (private collection)

terrace of Radic's house at Punta Pite is equally unbound, it creates a more dangerous edge than the cliffs on the site in part because the expectation of a liminal construction today is that it creates a safe enclosure. But it is precisely this unbound edge that unveils the wildness of the place, greeting visitors and inviting them to become enveloped in its nature.

The approach to the residence is deliberately gradual and composed with the intention of slowly revealing its various parts. Arriving at the terrace, cars are parked unceremoniously alongside the basalts, and visitord wander through the collection, perhaps pausing to admire the way the changing light emphasizes a previously unnoticed feature. The promontory in which this house is inserted provides the opportunity for shifting views and foci, all the while having the sea directly in front. Switching direction, the visitor descends another 3 meters, this time laterally, along a ramp that leads to another terrace, a ledge perched above the bluff and just below the hillside from which one can gain access to either the main living area or the lap pool. From here, steep steps take the visitor further down to the children's house, 40 meters below the point the site entry and to the edge of the sea. The guest wing is situated under the entry terrace beyond the main living areas of the house, and can also be accessed directly from the other side of the terrace behind one of the bounding walls. The buildings themselves amplify the existing topographic edges, and the site is traversed with stairways and ramps to explore these edge conditions. As a consequence, the compound heightens the awe one feels for the natural power of the place, and for the individual's small scale and fragility in the face of nature's immensity. However, more than just confrontation, the house also affords respite and haven from the site's harshness – the heat of the sun and the power of the ocean – and a meditative vantage point from which to experience the surrounding vastness with a sense of serenity.

A 90-meter diagonal line is drawn across the building site that both binds the compound's constituent parts together and delineates the distinction between them. Sometimes in the middle of the building, sometimes marking an edge, this line is most evident as the moment where the paving pattern changes. The seaward side is more refined, and pavers are set tightly together, whereas the inland side finds the pavers set further apart to allow the site's natural vegetation to regain a firm presence within the borders of the complex — constructed ground where the vista is most present and intertwined assembly where the building meets the hillside. Although relatively inconspicuous in photographs taken shortly after construction was completed, it isn't hard to imagine the rich landscape that will arise once the natural vegetation is allowed to regain its hold, and the distinction between the two worlds becomes more apparent. While traversing the compound, visitors are continually crossing back and forth between a more refined architectural world where composed building frames vista and landscape, and a rougher one where landscape and building are more palpably intertwined.

The polsed masses of the three components of the residence — the main house, the lap pool, and the children's house — are treated similarly, each precariously balanced and offering as uninterrupted views of the sea as possible.

Radic ensures such immediacy by, for instance, placing the window frame to the main living/dining room below the floor level and by constructing a large shadow-creating overhang, so that the onlooker has a sense of not being contained by any protection. Further, the exterior walkway along each room of the main house is left without a handrail, as are all other ramps and stairs. The view from the main living room of the children's house is framed merely by tectonic slabs. The significantly lower siting of the children's house, placing it intimately close to the highest waves, is fitting for the youth's capacity for dare.

The exposed concrete construction is omnipresent on the exterior, and often left unclad on the interior, such as in the living room, for example. Wooden floors and walls are more extensive in the bedroom areas, with the most luxurious finishes found in the bathrooms: here travertine lines all surfaces including the ceiling and forms even the washbasins. Graduating from rawness of the exterior public areas to the refined finishes in the spaces for personal sanitation, the applied finishes show a clear strategy.

In discussing architecture as an act of settlement, Dutch monk and architect Dom H. Van der Laan writes: "For the foot, the surface of the sandal represents a little piece of soft ground, whereas the underside acts as a toughened foot in relation to the ground. In the same way the inside of the house is for man a piece of habitable environment, while on the outside, where it confronts nature, it stands for a fortified human existence." Thus, between the two extreme terms of man and nature, the house appears as a reconciling element that enables man to maintain himself within nature.

Of course, any building, in some sense, reconciles its user to the environment. But for Radic, the role of enablement that Van der Laan describes is not an incidental concern, but rather the overarching agenda. Moreover, the experience of the Punta Pite house is also an incitement to re-envision the primary experiences of its place. Through the experience of this house, essential, raw qualities of the circumstance are omnipresent and more clearly framed. One enters the site with the sense that everything is readily apparent and laid out in full view, only to later realize that as the house unfolds, it reveals unbeknownst perspectives and insights. The winding entry sequence alternately removes the visitor from the omnipresent landscape, only to reintroduce it piece by piece in punctuated, pointed ways. The singular stillness of the water in the cantilevered lap pool, for example, is a datum against which one perceives the calmness and the ferocity of the sea, as well as the vicissitudes of weather. The contained space, darkness, and singular view from the guest rooms underline through contrast the immensity and brightness of the horizon. The children's building resting precariously on the boulders below the bluff, at the edge of the high water-line, reminds us of tremendous timber washed ashore from some past and violent storm. Completely open on both sides, it is like a lens that collapses the full immensity of the sea against the raw physicality of the rock cliff behind. The experience of Radic's Punta Pite house requires time, and the environment that he creates provokes the kind of reflective possibilities that Friedrich's painting highlights. It is a provisional building, always in flux with its circumstance, variously cloaked or exposed, and acting as an incitement to tread the earth with newfound wonder. Like the sandal, Radic's Punta Pite house is an architecture that once experienced seems both poignant and self-evident, but prior to its invention, unimaginable.

In comparison to other memorable vacation houses, Radic's Punta Pite residence retains the character of its site without overwhelming its architecture with sophistication or urbane elegance. It is a character of reality that constructs a world in the spirit of the place;

it is both a rough and raw beauty, distilled through art and architecture. Seen in relation to Eileen Gray's E.1027 at Roquebrune on the French Cotes d'Azure (1926-29), one of the first modern purpose, built vacation houses, the house at Punta Pite essentially distinguishes between architecture and furniture. Gray's design provides a degree of compact, steamer-inspired comfort that sets itself apart from the site. Less extravagant in its spatial extent, E.1027 is immodestly lean. The invention of multi-use furniture, such as built-in cupboards, equals that of the cabinetry of luxury steamers and railway carriages. For the pioneers of modern maritime sojourns, the design of these early houses carried with them the spirit of the picnic: a compacted translocation of urban luxury. In contrast, with the house at Punte Pite, built some eighty years after E.1027, there is no need to mimic the cabinetry of luxury transit or to emphasize the means of reaching the coast — from Santiago de Chilé to the coast is a two hour drive. Rather, here the rawness of the waterfront's edge is synthesized with the house, and through its experience, the visitor cannot evade nature's serenity or its wildness.

Like most waterfront houses, E.1027 is recognizably a house, even if wrapped in a modern "naval" architecture. The Villa Malaparte by Adalberto Libera and Curzio Malaparte at Punto Masullo near Capri (1938-42) already shifts from the expressive mode to a fusion of figure and ground: it is simultaneously a crouched animal and a grand terrace. One could argue that the Casa Vittorio by Lluís Clotet and Oscar Tusquests on the Ila de Pantelleria in Sicily (1972-75) extends this same strategy to its logical conclusion through a series of terraces with flat roofs that enclose habitable spaces. The set of rudimentary, almost archaic pergola in their picturesque composition echo the rocky topography, while also allowing the onlooker to recall the ruins of ancient archaeological sites, even the distant Temple of Poseidon on Cape Sounion (ca. 440 BC).

Thus in the discourse of waterfront houses, the Punta Pite house could be said to occupy a position somewhere between the Villa Malaparte and the Casa Vittoria — in part figure and in part ground. The house occupies as much a clear position in the discourse as it does in its precise siting: on the raw edge.

Clotet & Tusquets, Casa Vittoria (1972-5), Pantelleria, Italy, photo courtesy Lluís Clotet

Cape Sounion, Aegean Sea, Greece, with the ruins of the Temple of Poseidon (c. 440 BC)

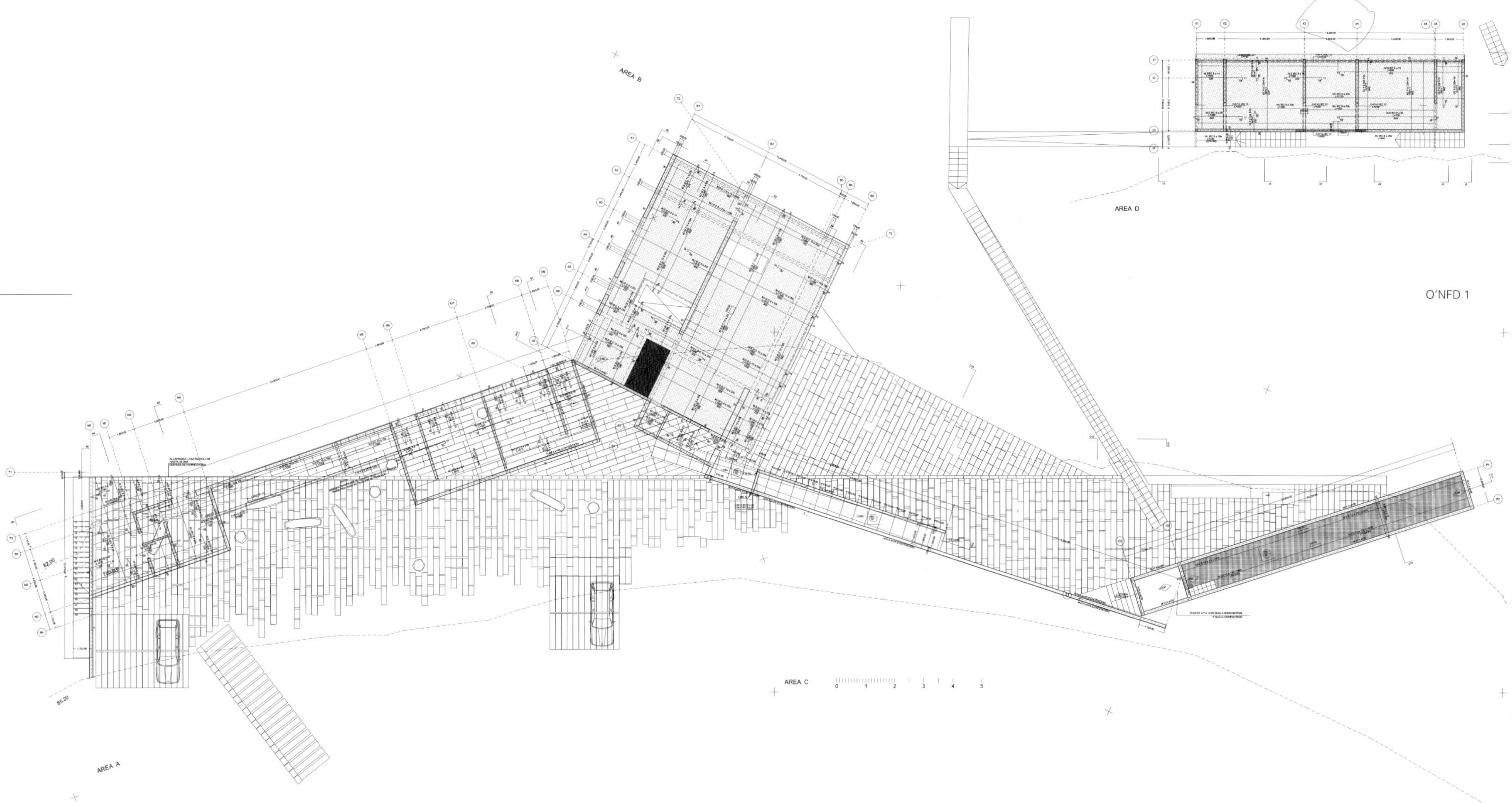
AREA B
AREA D
O'NFD 1
AREA C
0 1 2 3 4 5
AREA A

House at Punta Pite

Smiljan Radic

The House at Punta Pite was constructed as a weekend house on a plot of 1.5 hectare in Papudo almost two hours from Santiago, the capital of Chilé. The design of the project took eight months, and its construction two years.

To allow for greater flexibility, among other things, in the periods of the house's use, my project proposes the display of the interior program of 400m2 at the length and width of the plot and in the middle of the uncomfortable nature, with the understanding that the diverse and distinct situations of the geography will help characterize each of the interiors.

A highway that joins various coastal points, marks the upper margin of the plot. Approximately 40 meters above sea level and on one of the highway's curves emerges a vehicle path to access the site. This path crosses the upper part of the site on a diagonal, constituted by a hillside with a soft slope and vegetation of native bushes. The path ends in an extensive lookout point of 40 lineal meters, where cars are parked. The lookout is occupied by 11 basalts that are dispersed over a pavement of concrete tiles-in-the-rough that were fabricated during the construction. These large rocks, that form part of an art installation by the sculptor Marcela Correa, were brought from a quarry 450 kilometers away from the plot, and each one weights between three and nine tons. The installation intends not only to hide or "veil" the house, as requested by the owners, but also to bury it definitely under a physical and temporal weight.

Under this lookout point, at which a geographically pronounced change is produced by a slope and the vegetation in the area between the hillside of the access and the ravine packed with cactus, a major part of the program of the house is developed, displayed on a length of 95 lineal meters.

A central ramp unites the lookout point with the domestic terrace. On one of its extremes is a pool and the outdoor cooking area, and on the other, the areas of the family room, dining room, kitchen, master bedroom, and bathrooms. At the end of this pavilion and behind a retaining wall are the guest rooms and the service area, which are accessed through an exterior corridor that skirts the crest of the ravine.

Eighteen meters below an accumulation of granite that rolled from the seaward hillside marks the end of the ravines. Here, immediately tangential to them, boxed between a natural headland and the ravines behind it, is a simple volume

with the program for the owner's children: the bedrooms, bathrooms, family room, and heating stove. Each of these programs — the parent's, guest's and children's — is composed of symmetrical modules connected between each other by 800m2 of terraces and exterior ramps elevated over the level of the natural terrain.

All of the interior areas establish a unique relationship with the sea as a result of their shape and positioning. The central pavilion is suspended over the ocean, and the carpentry of its windows, its pavements, and its projecting frontal position with respect to the elevation help to make this interior understood as a kind of raft. The guest rooms and service rooms were projected as caves buried in the hillside, safeguarding a certain distance from the abrupt ravine they encircle. Finally, the children's bedrooms are dramatically in the sea, as close as possible to the line where the waves hit the rocks on stormy days.

Pite house will finish settling into its terrain in two or three more years, when the native vegetation has definitely recuperated and the concrete pavements and their grooves are inhabited by pasture.

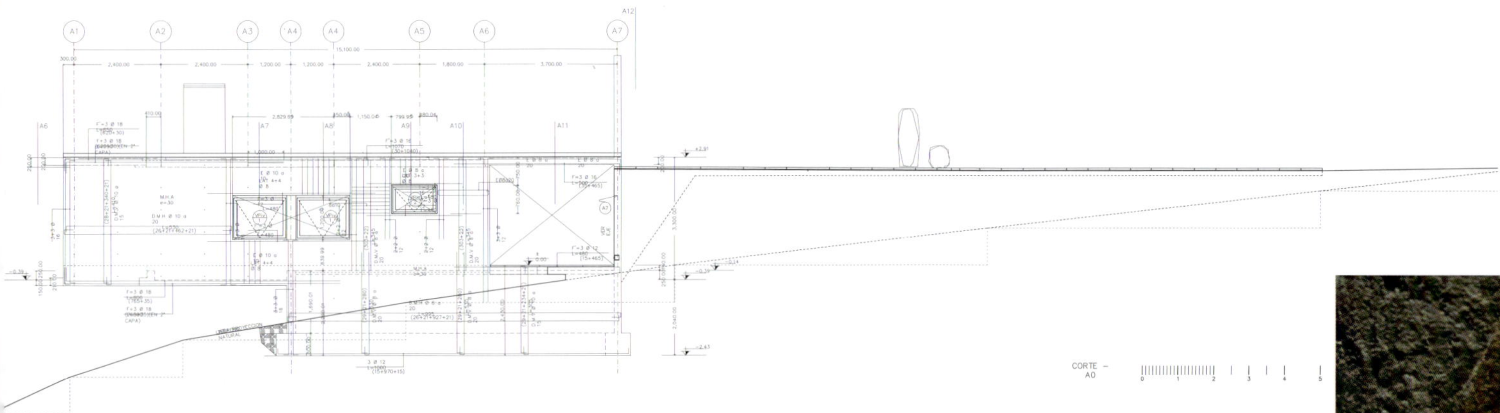

CORTE – AD

30

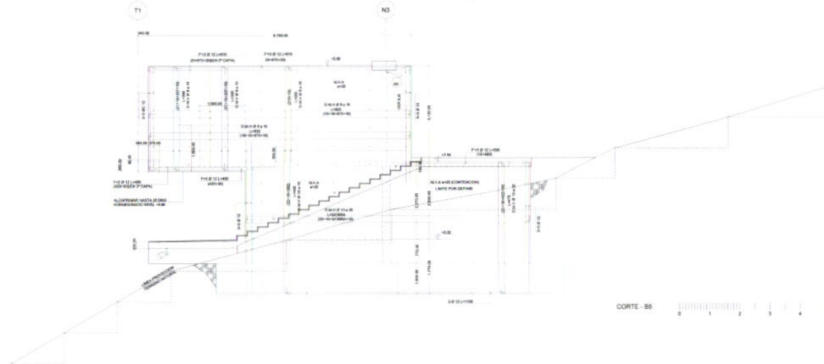

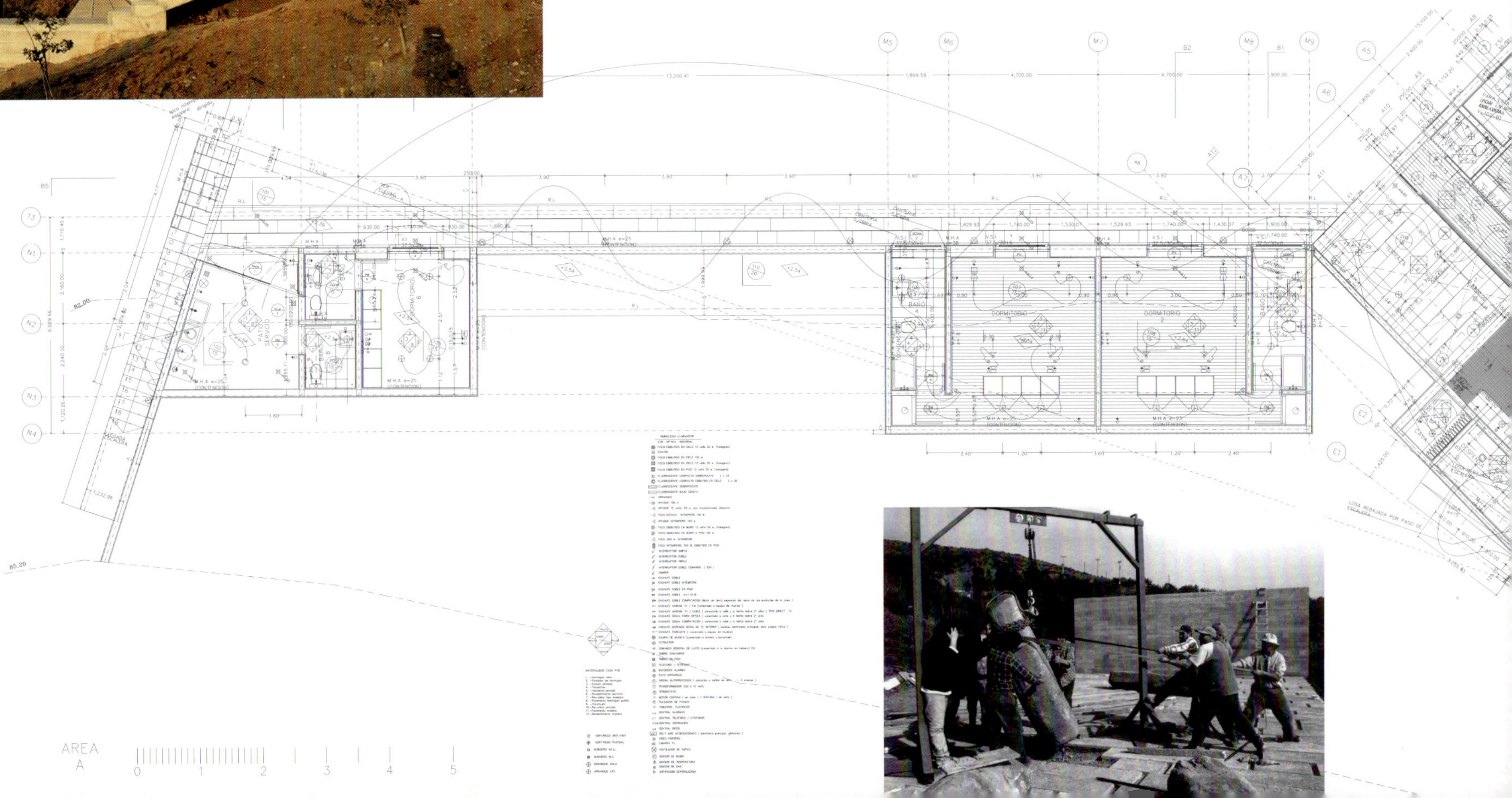

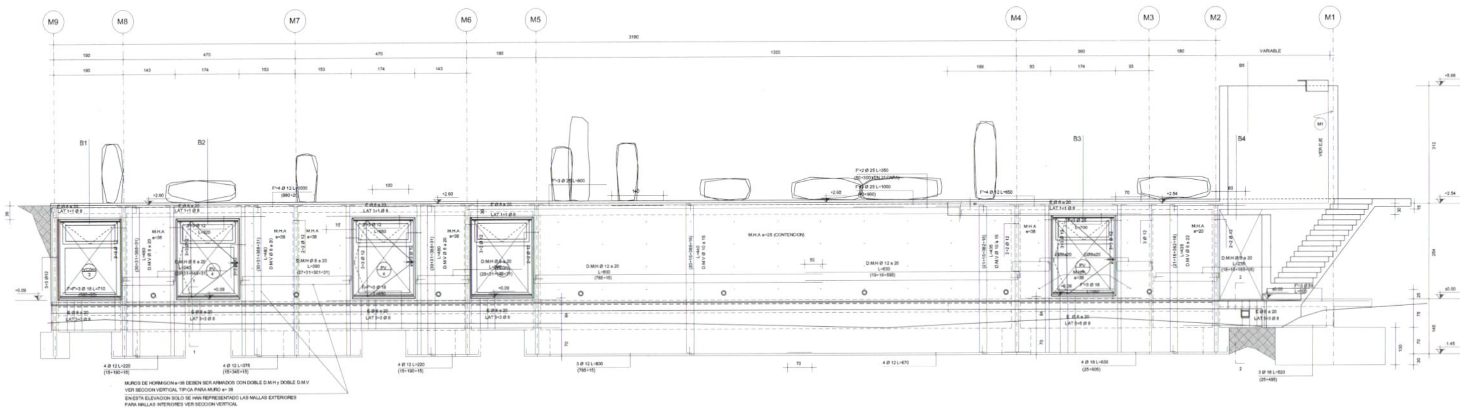

CORTE - A5

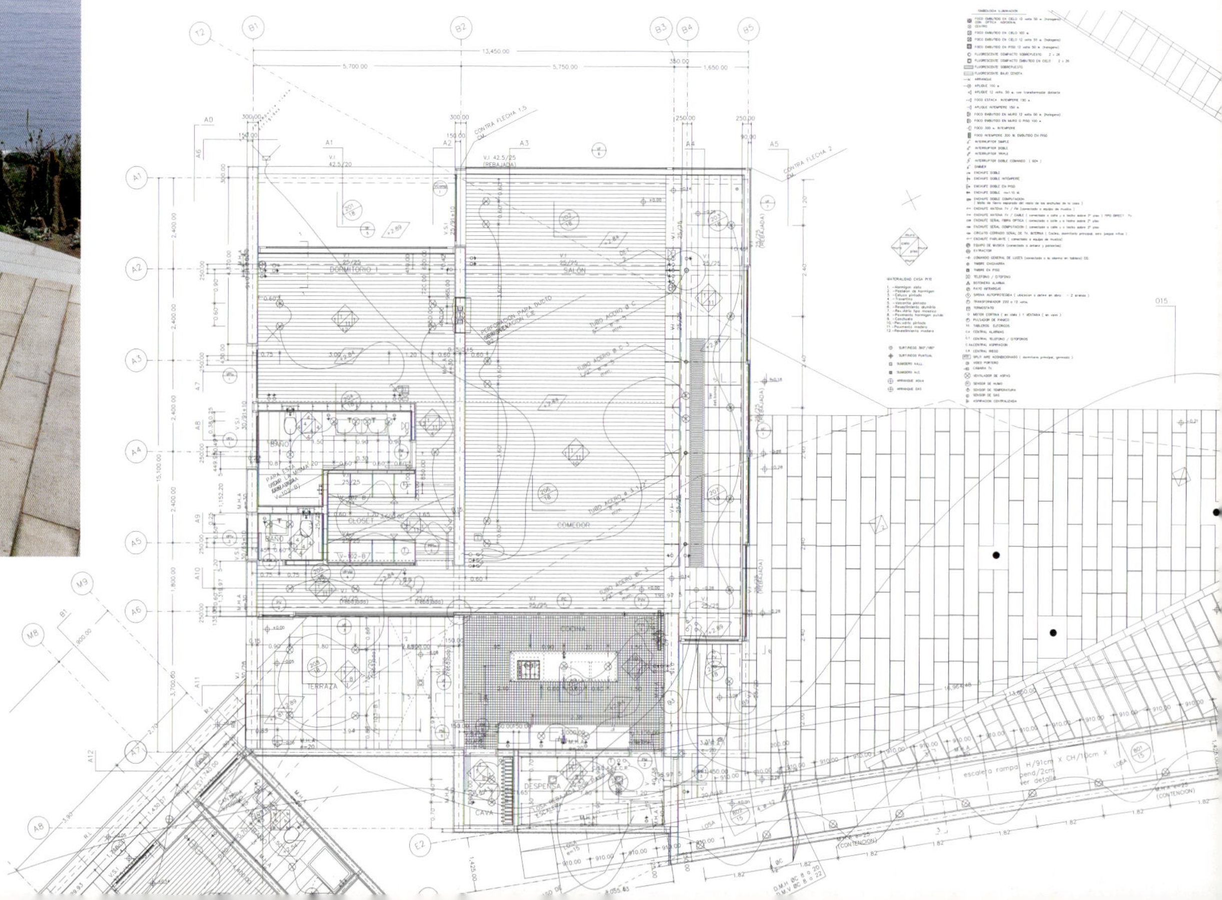

SALON
COMEDOR
COCINA
TERRAZA

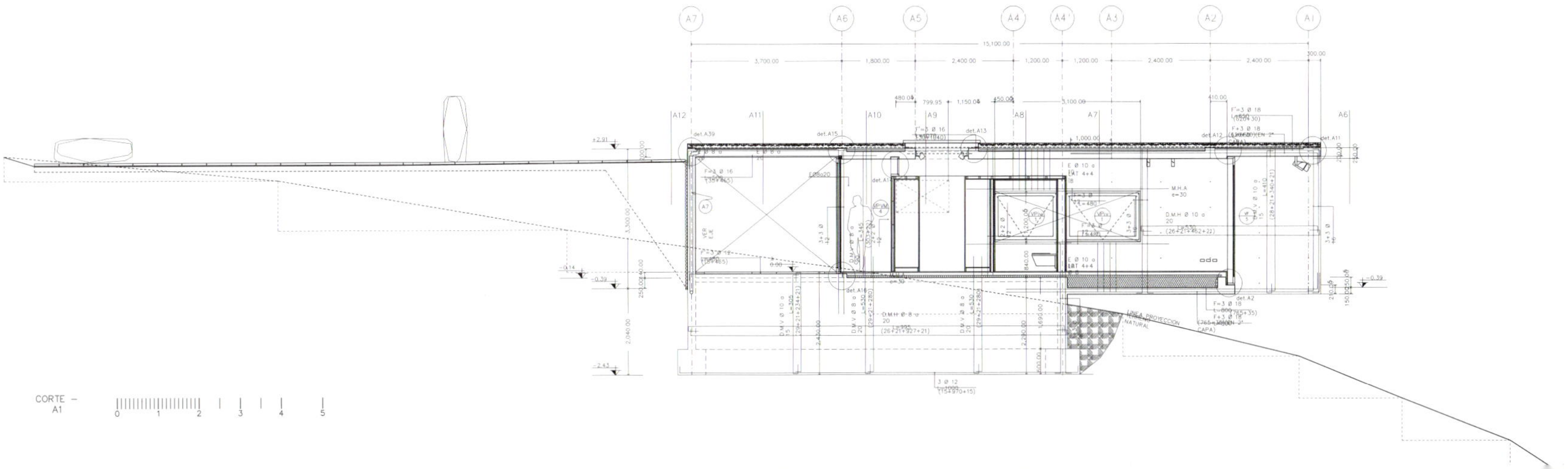

CORTE — A1

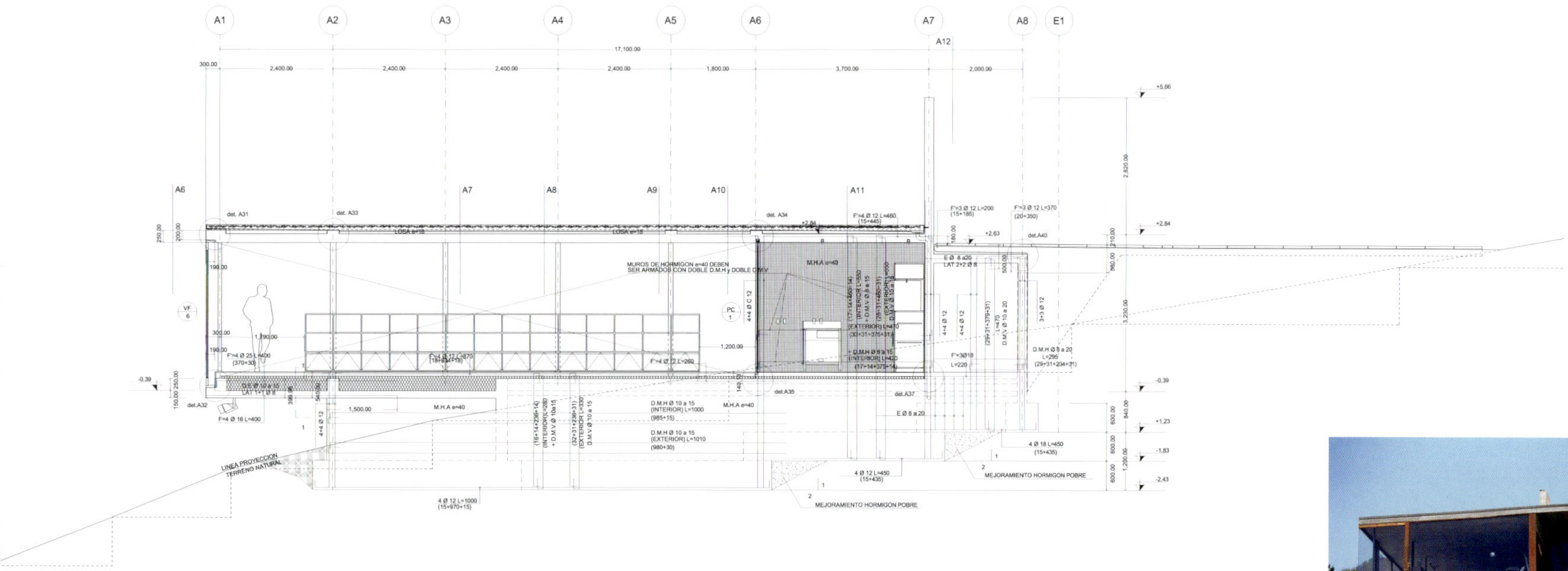
A1
A2
A3
A4
A5
A6
A7
A8
E1
A12
A6
A7
A8
A9
A10
A11

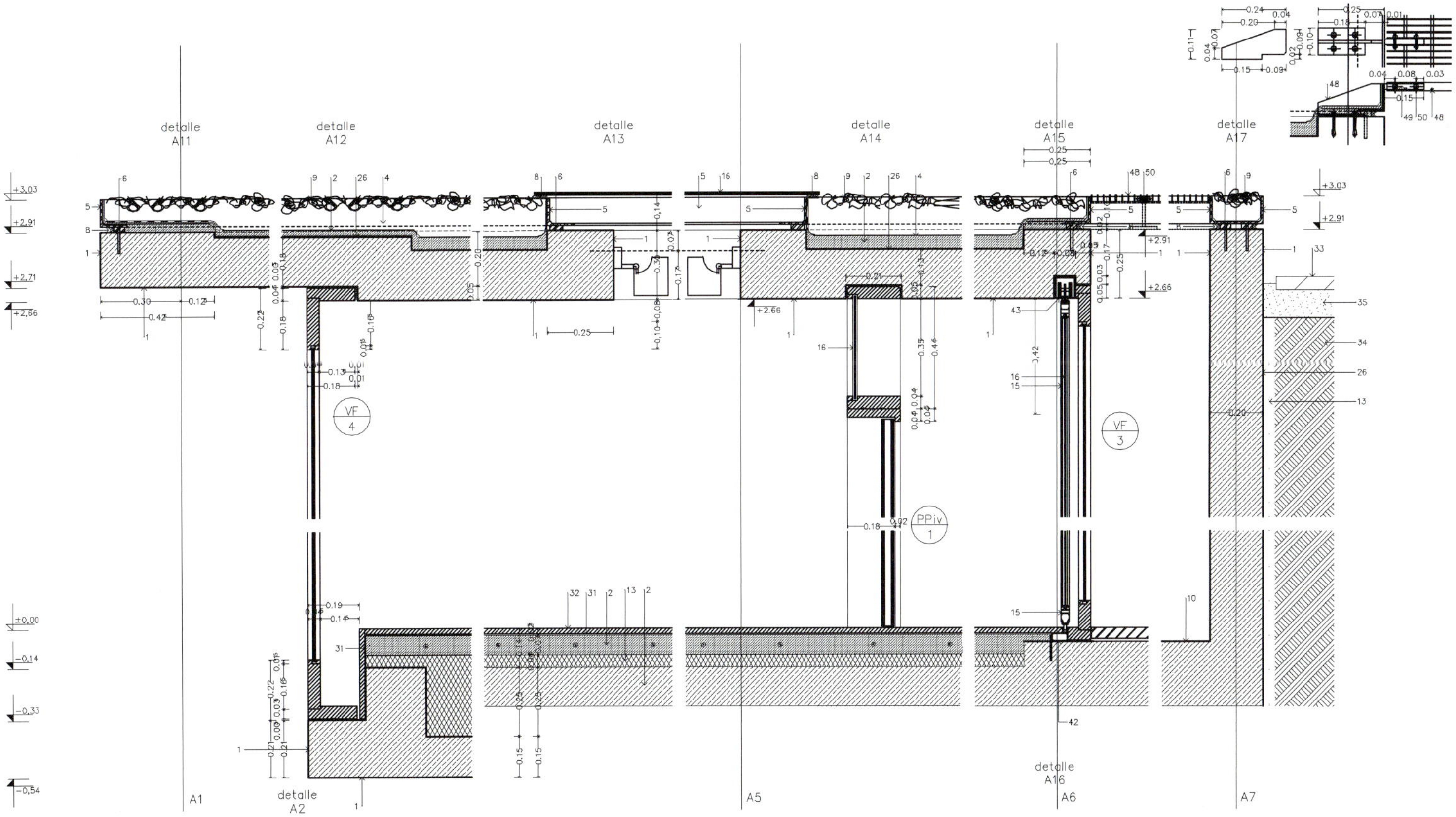

1 hormigón visto
2 sobrelosa hormigón
3 fe estructural asimét. s/c
4 membrana imperm. tipo 1
5 fe L 100x100x8 m
6 fe o 40x20x3 mm
7 fe barra 40x20
8 silicona estructural
9 relleno conchuela
10 pavimento hormigón pulido
11 rev. mad. machiemb. 20 mm esp.
12 madera aglomerada 15 mm
13 poliestireno expandido
14 revestimiento mosaico vidrio
15 ventana aluminio
16 vidrio 10 mm esp.
17 fe L 265x100x5 mm
18 fe I 265x5 mm
19 PVC 75 mm
20 Desague PVC 75 mm
21 cortina roller
22 perno hilti expansión
23 fe L 65x65x5 aza
24 AL 80x40x1.5 mm
25 membrana tipo 2
26 imperm. igol denso
27 junquillo fe 10x10mm
28 terciado marino 15 mm
29 revestimiento aluminio
30 vidrio pintado 10 mm
31 pegamento madera
32 pavimento madera 1x4"
33 pavimento baldosas hormigón
34 terreno compactado
35 arena c/fragua superficial
36 revestimiento aluminio
37 fe o 50x50x4 mm
38 fe L 50x50x4 mm
39 fe o 60x30x3 mm
40 PVC 100 mm
41 fe – 10 mm esp.
42 fe o 60x30x3 mm
43 riel ducasse 70x76 cms. 1000 kg.
44 estuco p/pintar
45 rev. travertino 20 mm.
46 pav. madera 1x4"
47 guardapolvo fe 30x30x2 ac.inox
48 parrilla electroforjada
49 fe o 20x20x2 mm.
50 perno sujeccion parrilla
51 pletina e:10 mm.

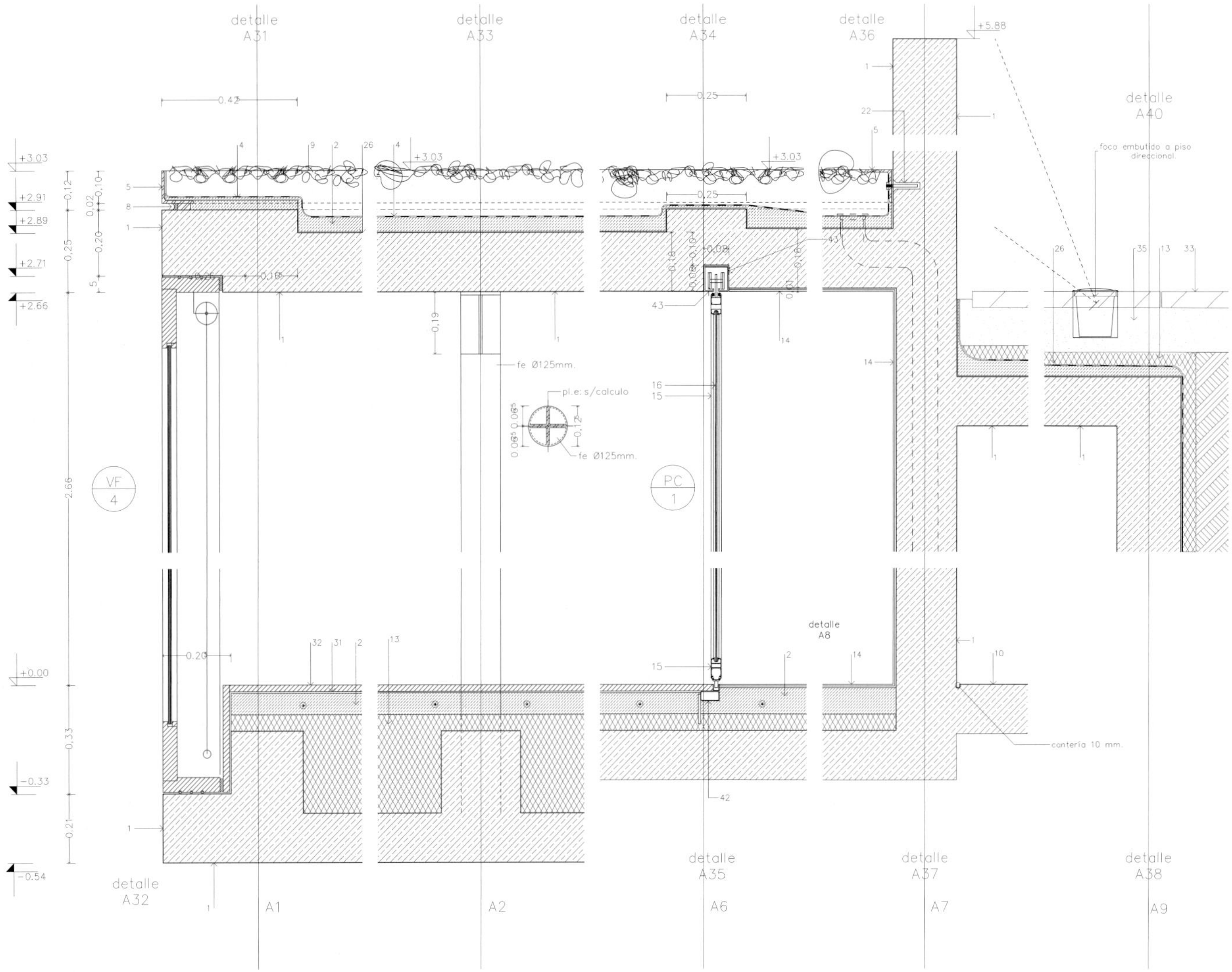

- 1 hormigón visto
- 2 sobrelosa hormigón
- 3 fe estructural asimét. s/c
- 4 membrana imperm. tipo 1
- 5 fe L 100x100x8 m
- 6 fe o 40x20x3 mm
- 7 fe barra 40x20
- 8 silicona estructural
- 9 relleno conchuela
- 10 pavimento hormigón pulido
- 11 rev. mad. machiemb. 20 mm esp.
- 12 madera aglomerada 15 mm
- 13 poliestireno expandido
- 14 revestimiento mosaico vidrio
- 15 ventana aluminio
- 16 vidrio 10 mm esp.
- 17 fe L 265x100x5 mm
- 18 fe I 265x5 mm
- 19 PVC 75 mm
- 20 Desague PVC 75 mm
- 21 cortina roller
- 22 perno hilti expansión
- 23 fe L 65x65x5 aza
- 24 AL 80x40x1.5 mm
- 25 membrana tipo 2
- 26 imperm. igol denso
- 27 junquillo fe 10x10mm
- 28 terciado marino 15 mm
- 29 revestimiento aluminio
- 30 vidrio pintado 10 mm
- 31 pegamento madera
- 32 pavimento madera 1x4"
- 33 pavimento baldosas hormigón
- 34 terreno compactado
- 35 arena c/fragua superficial
- 36 revestimiento aluminio
- 37 fe o 50x50x4 mm
- 38 fe L 50x50x4 mm
- 39 fe o 60x30x3 mm
- 40 PVC 100 mm
- 41 fe – 10 mm esp.
- 42 fe o 60x30x3 mm
- 43 riel ducasse 70x76 cms. 1000 kg.
- 44 estuco p/pintar
- 45 rev. travertino 20 mm.
- 46 pav. madera 1x4"
- 47 guardapolvo fe 30x30x2 ac.inox
- 48 parrilla electroforjada
- 49 fe o 20x20x2 mm.
- 50 perno sujeccion parrilla
- 51 pletina e:10 mm.

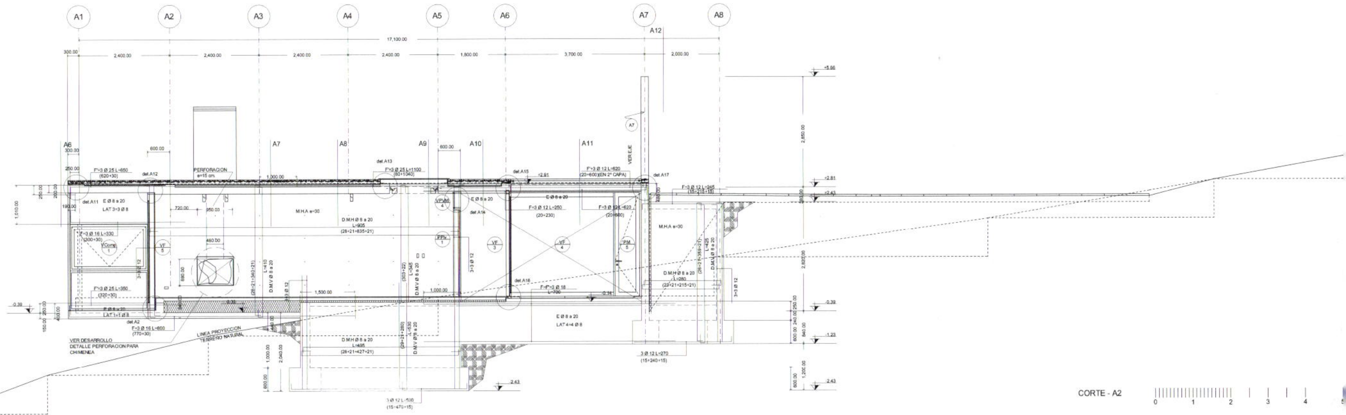
CORTE - A2

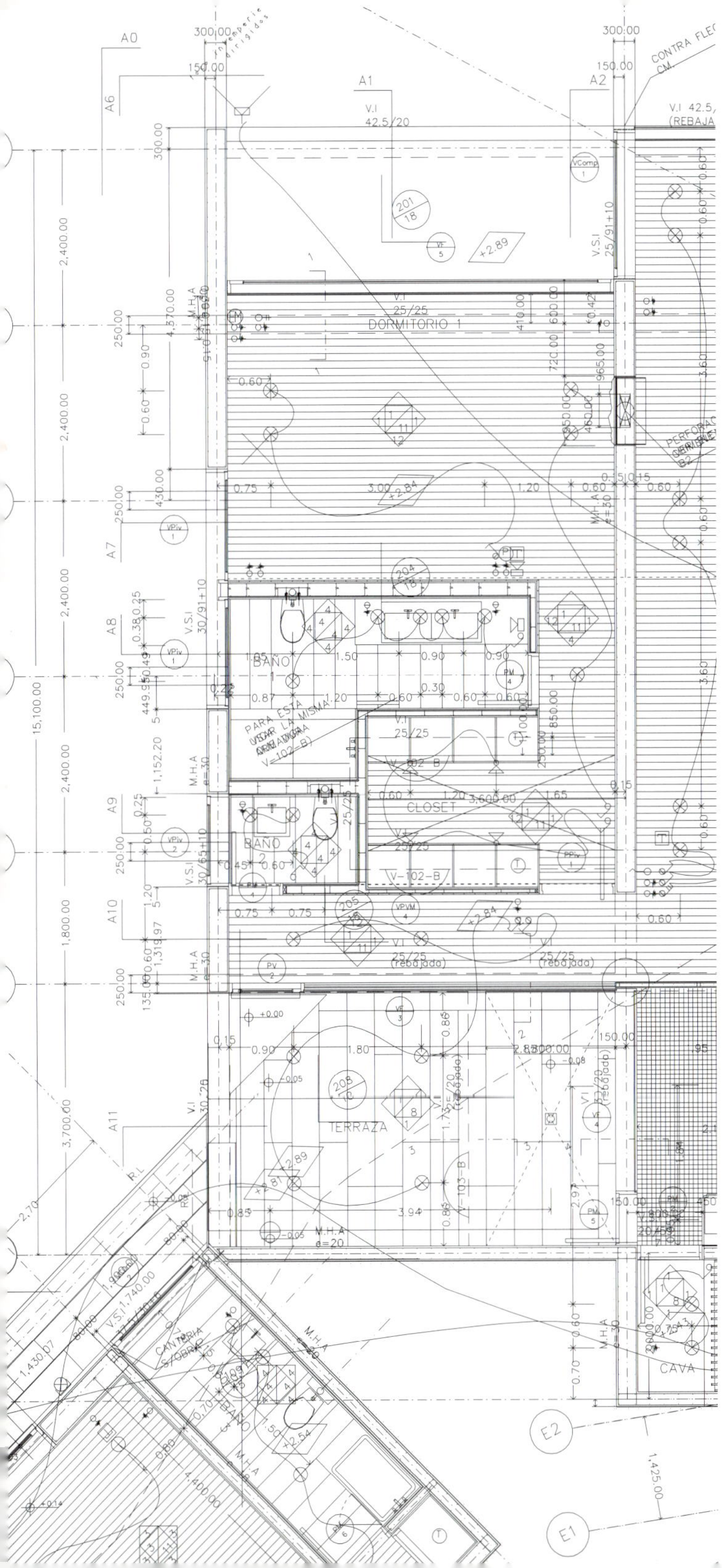
DORMITORIO 1
BAÑO
CLOSET
TERRAZA
CAVA

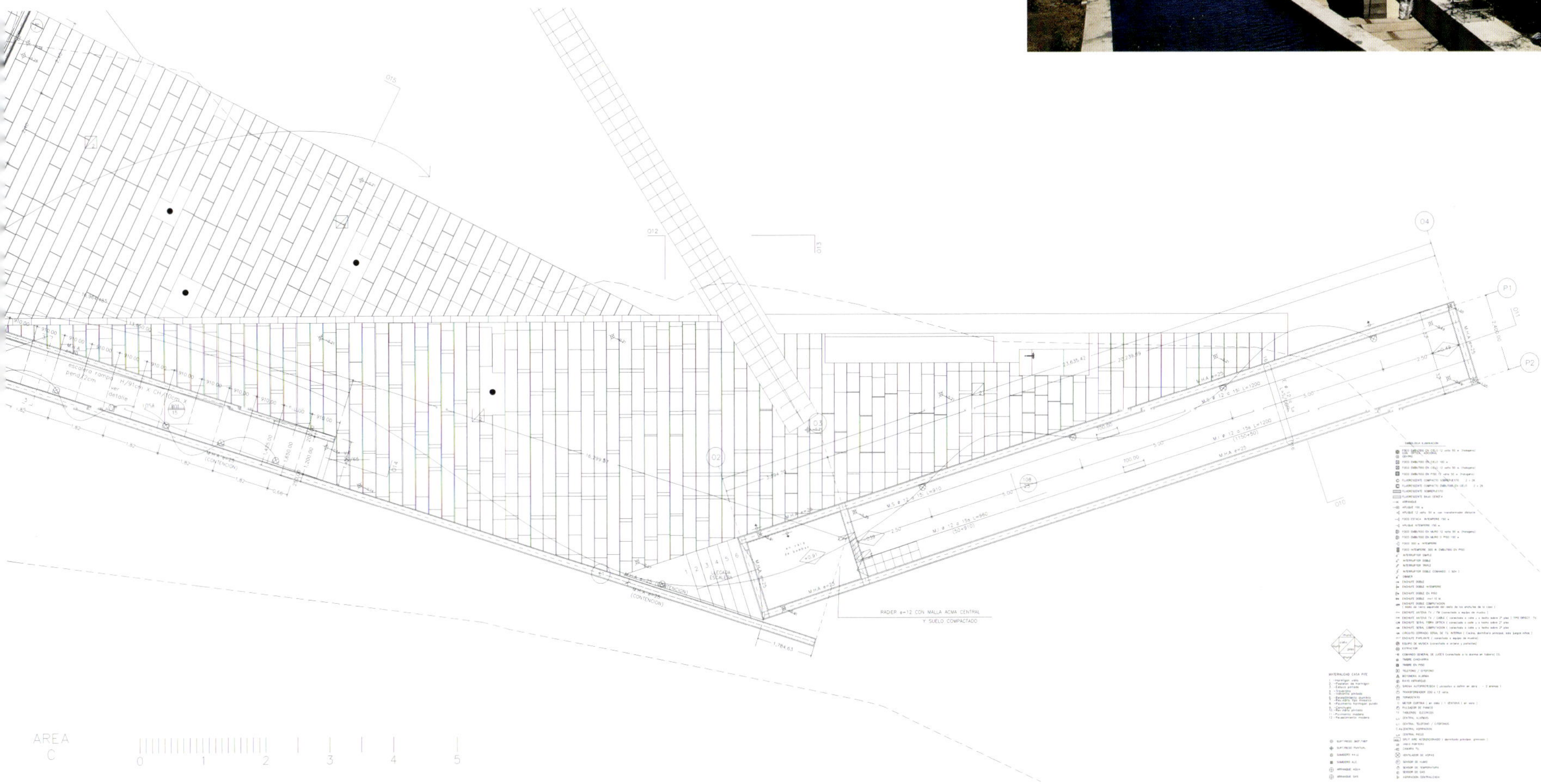
RADIER e=12 CON MALLA ACMA CENTRAL
Y SUELO COMPACTADO
AREA
C
0
1
2
3
4
5

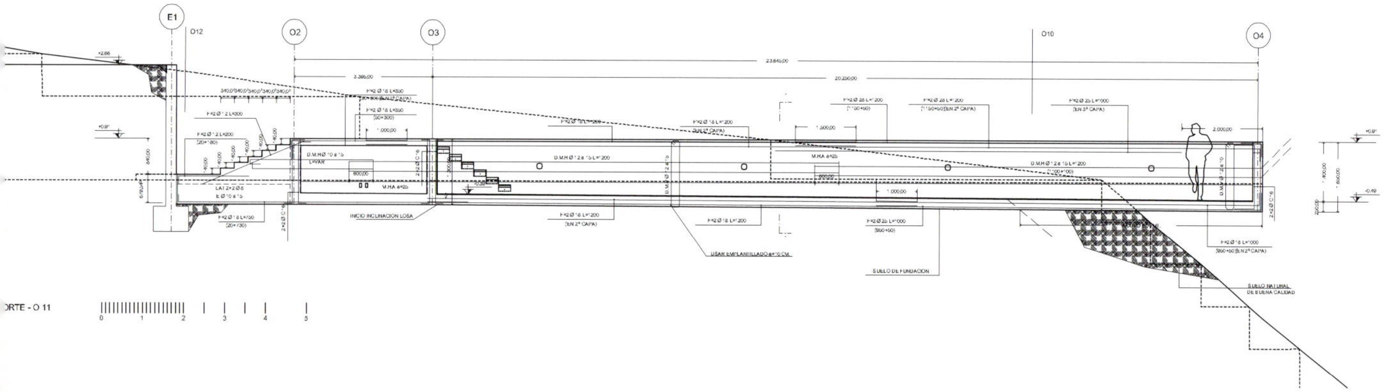
E1
O12
O2
O3
O10
O4
ORTE - O 11

O'NFD 1

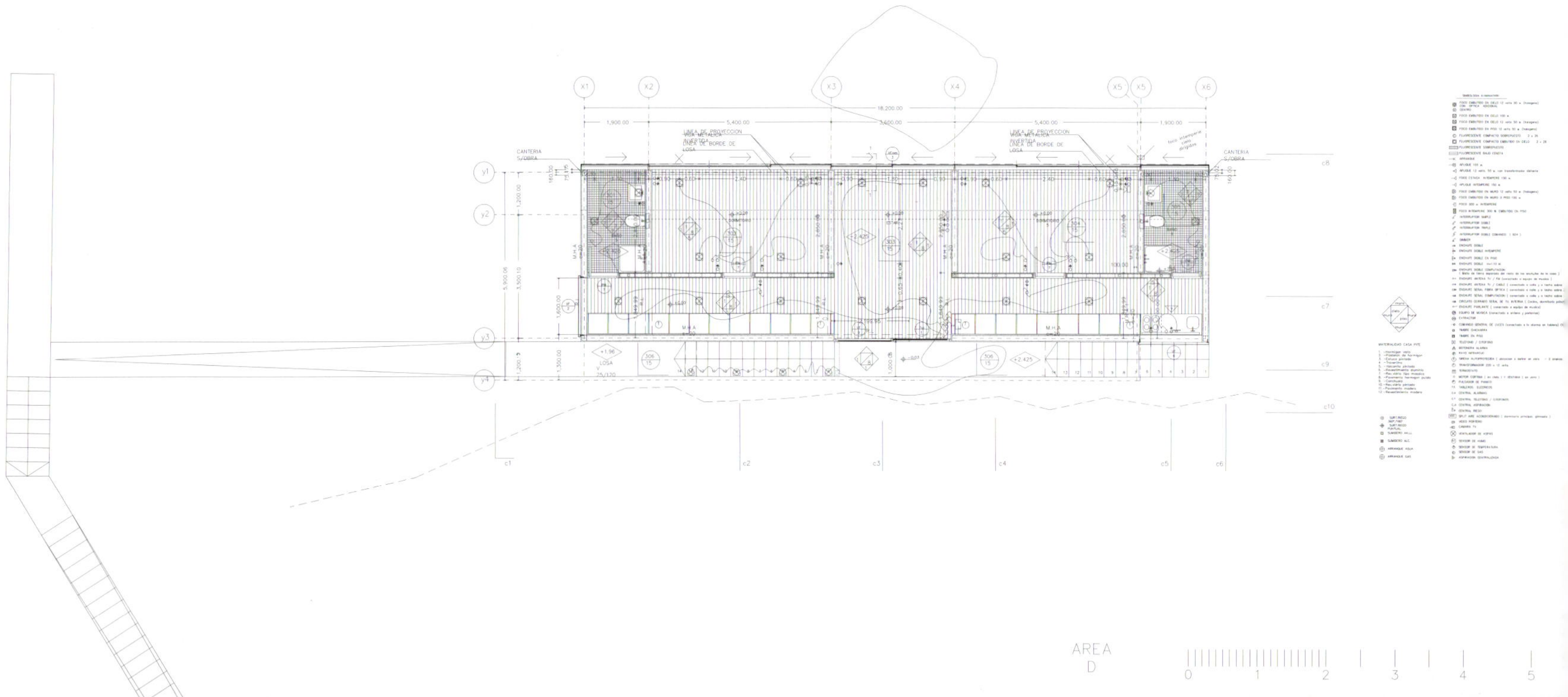

AREA
D

0 1 2 3 4 5

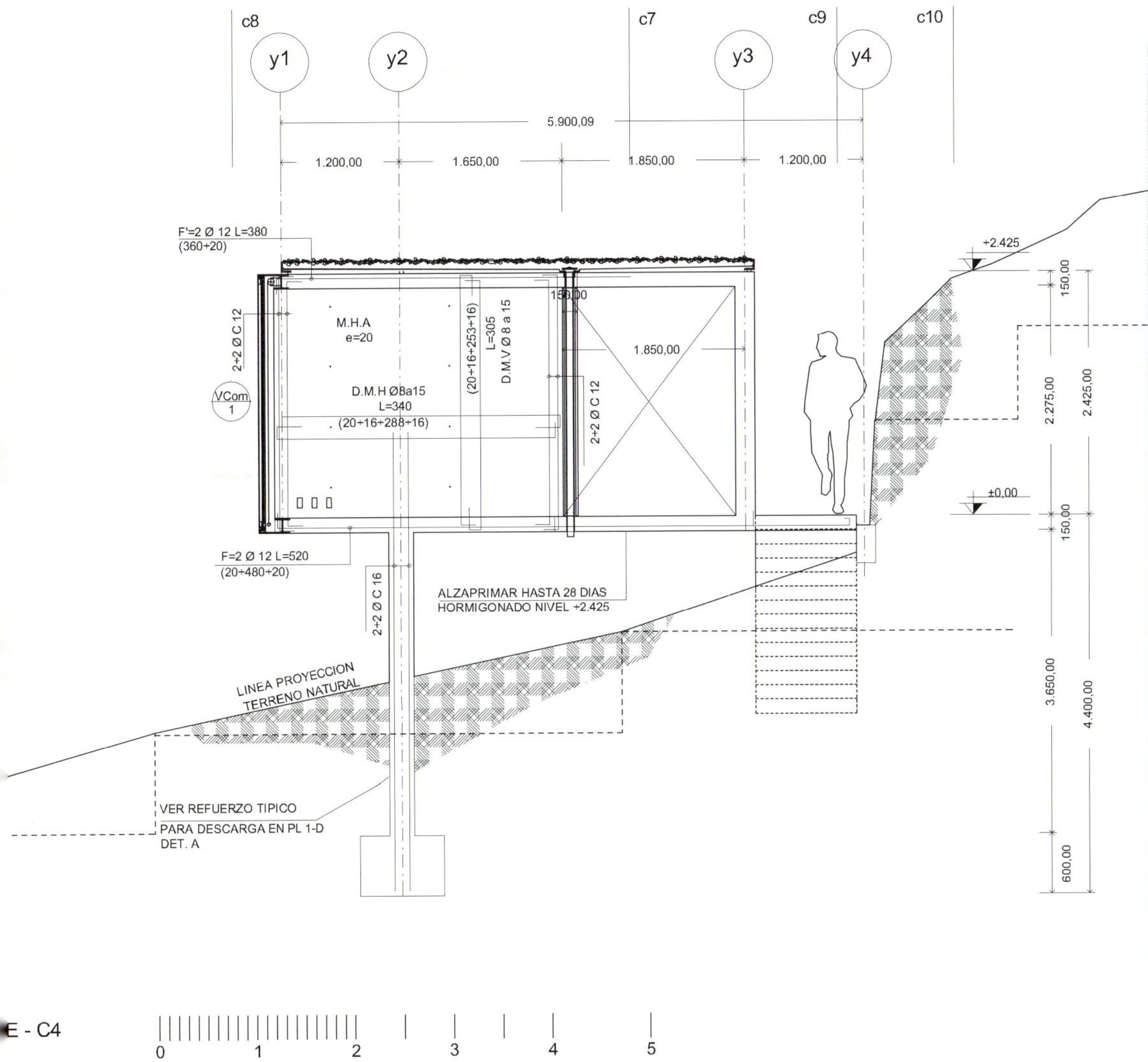
c8
c7
c9
c10
y1
y2
y3
y4
5.900,09
1.200,00
1.650,00
1.850,00
1.200,00
F'=2 Ø 12 L=380
(360+20)
M.H.A
e=20
D.M.H Ø8a15
L=340
(20+16+288+16)
(20+16+253+16)
L=305
D.M.V Ø 8 a 15
2+2 Ø C 12
VCom
1
150,00
1.850,00
+2.425
±0,00
2.275,00
2.425,00
150,00
F=2 Ø 12 L=520
(20+480+20)
2+2 Ø C 16
ALZAPRIMAR HASTA 28 DIAS
HORMIGONADO NIVEL +2.425
LINEA PROYECCION
TERRENO NATURAL
3.650,00
4.400,00
VER REFUERZO TIPICO
PARA DESCARGA EN PL 1-D
DET. A
600,00
E - C4
0
1
2
3
4
5

O'NFD 1

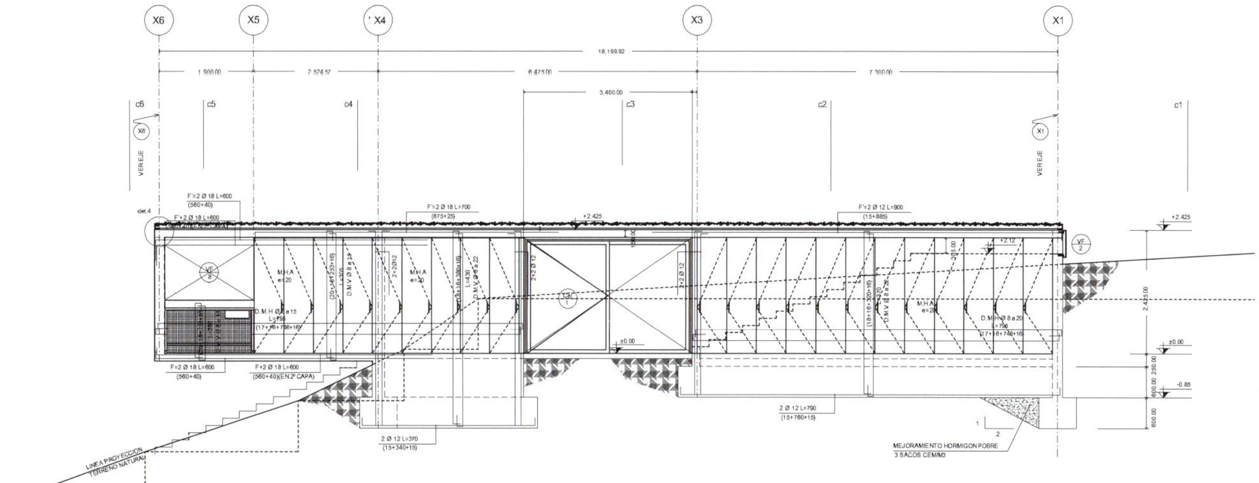

CORTE - C7

O'NFD 1

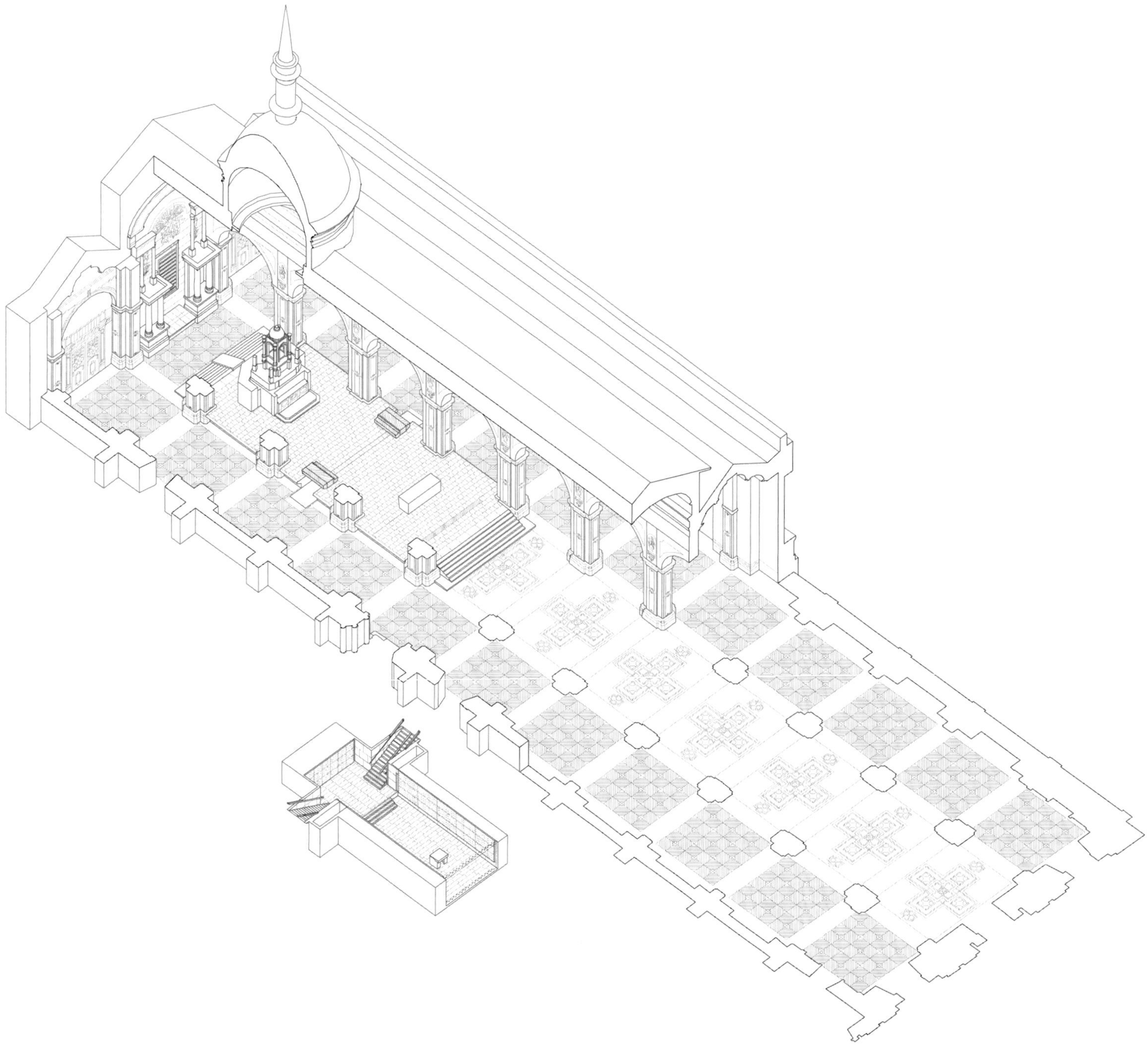

Crypt in the Cathedral of Santiago de Chilé, 1999-2006

Rodrigo Pérez de Arce

Above and Below

Kevin Alter, Wilfried Wang

Churches have become so familiar to Western culture that their ideal typical form is well embedded in the mind of any individual who has grown up in a Christian context. Thus, churches appear to have something of a timeless, unquestioned logic. However, like any other product of civilization, the parts of a church — from the nave, transept, and altar, to the spires and so forth — constitute an amalgam of culturally, or perhaps better spiritually, charged spatial elements, that have origins in a variety of ritualistic practices. The case of the crypt is no different. An important root of the Christian crypt is found in the Roman catacombs, although catacombs themselves date further back to Ukrainian and Russian underground mines. Indeed, underground burial chambers in catacomb-like hollows can be traced back to the Bronze Age (3500 – 2000 BC), and some of the most complex and impressive examples have been found in the Altay Mountains and in the Caucasus.

Early Christians are said to have gathered in the safety of the Roman catacombs to bury their dead and to worship in secret. According to legend, the Basilica of St. Peter's was built on top of the grave of the Apostle Peter; more specifically, the altar of the basilica was said to have been built directly on top of Peter's grave. The modern crypt and altar thus preserve the legend of these times of persecution: the transformed catacomb became the crypt in which the followers of St. Peter — that is to say, the representative leaders of the local ecclesiastic organization — were laid to rest. The fixed altar became "the living stone" upon which the Eucharist is performed.

In continuing this privileged burial practice and its associated space and location, homage is being paid to the origins of the Christian church. The biblical alliteration to St. Peter, in which "Petrus" is equated with the rock upon which the church will be built, establishes an incontrovertible command for the entire Christian church.

Such legends, memories, references, and rituals form the matrix in which one of the most unusual commissions was set: the construction of a crypt and the associated redesign of the presbytery and altar for the Cathedral of Santiago de Chilé. Rodrigo Pérez de Arce won the architectural competition for the project in 2002, and his design was intensively developed in close liaison with both the extensive church authorities and the National Monuments Board; the project was executed from 2005 to 2007 while numerous details were still being discussed concurrently.

Whereas conventionally, churches have been built from the crypt upwards, Santiago de Chilé's cathedral only had a rudimentary underground burial chamber (during the preparatory excavations for the new crypt, among others, the remains of the controversial politician Diego Portales Palazuelos (1793-1837) were found). Thus the task of installing a crypt post facto, so to speak, is not only unusual, it is fraught with such problems as: considerations over the "construction" of a historical reference that would not pretend to create a false history as a result of the choice of any one architectural language; the manifestation of a modern corporeality that would embody both Christian values as well as a credible and comprehensible architectural idea that sets itself apart from the neo-Baroque of the cathedral; the interpretation of current guidelines from the Second Vatican Council regarding the quality of the design, as well as the position of the altar; not to mention the mundane issue of constructing among the foundations of a building while it is in constant use.

At the Cathedral of Santiago de Chilé, the height of the raised presbytery is related to the base of the shafts of the adjacent piers and to the viewing angles from the congregation within the nave. Thus, the new finished floor-level of the presbytery meets the underside of the central panels of the nave piers, thereby preserving the unity of the moldings. As detailed, the new plane of the presbytery is given a lid-like appearance by the bull-nosed edge profile to the presbytery's sides. This detail characterizes the ground of the presbytery as an idealized slab, alluding to the lid of a coffin, while also creating a more abstracted, modern version of the adjacent moldings of the piers. The height of the raised crypt is then matched to the socle of the piers. The slab's thickness is also made palpable by the two openings above the staircases as well as by the insertion of a large wooden beam, which is set flush with the floor of the presbytery and follows the pattern of the crypt's stepped ceiling. This wooden beam marks the position for the candidates for priesthood during the ordaining ceremony, acting as a physical mnemonic of the cycle of life and a tangible connection with the forefathers of the church.

The floor-level of the crypt was determined in turn by the inclination of the stairs and the available clearance between the nave's piers. A separation between the burial chambers of the worldly and religious leaders is created by lowering the main crypt space by a further three steps. This is the final resting place for the archbishops and deans. The grid like set of travertine panels, each panel in turn scored with dimples reminiscent of casting holes in concrete walls, are bolted to a steel sub-construction in each corner. This arrangement of the tombs provides just enough differentiation within each individual tomb to attain an identity; however, seen in relation to the grey stone floor, the black base of the grid of tombs and the flushness of the travertine panels, the two long sides of the crypt become uniform walls. Their flatness underlines the presence of the altar and the suspended figure of Christ.

Furthermore, the ubiquitous motif of the steps as used on the ceiling and walls becomes a second privileged formal element. These steps serve to remind the visitor of the unending cycle of life and death. To underline this continuity, the steps are also clad in travertine; however, thresholds such as planes of entry or changes in level are marked by massive timber lintels or steps. Pérez de Arce's opposition to the general tectonic condition of expressed travertine in a transitional setting is here underscored by the choice of a more modest material applied in a more monumental way.

All the detailing — whether the travertine cladding of the steps or the panels to the tombs, whether the wooden lintels or steps, or the carefully assembled handrails of steel and wood, or the granite altar — emphasizes the material reality. There is no pretence in the application of materials here. There is no "fake" here, a critique of the existing architecture of the Cathedral that Pérez de Arce has made on a number of instances.

Such matter-of-fact material presence, combined with the unusually large wooden elements, the massive altar, and the more metaphorical reading of the presbytery as a giant lid to the crypt, lays claim to a corporeal architecture that is first of itself, before being read as a representation for a religious ritual and its meaning in ecclesiastical history.

Beside the material presence of the components, the formal treatment of them as flush and polished pieces permits the new intervention to be read in distinction from the preexisting architecture, thereby documenting a further layer in the constructed sediment.

The resulting appearance of the new presbytery and crypt is a simultaneously calm and bold set of spaces and surfaces upon which, or in which, are placed honed furnishings. The surfaces, spaces, and objects are abstractions of their respective types; they have undergone a process of change, a transformation in time that has allowed them to arrive as refreshed symbols of the past. The altar and the choir's benches (doubling as the lintels to the crypt entrances) are inflected, highly polished parallelepipeds, thereby claiming their origin in the primitive and primary while also asserting their membership in the realm of the civilized. The presbytery is a stage for ritual; its new objects are silent, immovable participants in a choreography.

Seen from the nave, the novelty of the presbytery is hardly discernable. For this, Pérez de Arce's careful insertion of the large horizontal surface amongst the piers and the presence of the wide steps leading up to the new presbytery are just what they need to be. In that sense, a functionalist primitivism is already in place that in this instance synthesizes Pérez de Arce's interest in the development of modernist history, beginning with the Swiss stage designer Adolphe Appia's geometrized monumental landscapes (1911), Ludwig Mies van der Rohe's application of these ideas to the Weissenhofsiedlung (1927), and the brick houses for Lange and Esters in Krefeld (1931, 1932) and leading up to the Farnsworth House (1957) and the hauntingly sparse paintings by Giorgio de Chirico. In these various reductions of what a horizontal surface can be, the different artists and architects implicitly condense historic meanings. In this context, the way in which ground is materialized and denoted becomes the litmus test: Appia and de Chirico indicate large slabs; Mies van der Rohe either uses bricks or stone panels; Pérez de Arce has large marble slabs laid over the presbytery. Such are the detailing techniques that aid a return to essentials.

To the rear of the presbytery, one of the two earlier burial grounds of the cathedral has been marked by a large travertine ramp-like slab. Daylight entering through the newly opened grand west window illuminates the large travertine slab of the tomb. Rather than refilling the west window with a figurative composition of leaded glass, Pérez de Arce set a new rectangular glazing plane in front of the arched opening. Each cast glass panel creates a refractive pattern: arranged in vertical stripes they are alternatively grids of crosses and whorls. The church plans to place a statue of Diego Portales Palazuelos at the base of the window niche, an extraordinary gesture of honor firstly for a profane figure — after all, this is the termination of the east-west axis of a church — and secondly, for such a controversial character. With the window design, Pérez de Arce is using the Baroque technique of backlighting. While the immediate object of the statue will be prominently lit, the window has the capacity to project light further into the nave so much so that it will retrieve the plasticity of the historic tabernacle. The diffuse light casts this in a mild glow.

In contrast to many older crypts with shallow and narrow span vaults, and numerous stub columns, the crypt at the Cathedral of Santiago de Chilé appears generously grand, even lofty. The indirect lighting is integral to the space, providing subtle drama to the few figurative objects: statues and altar. With the emphasis on edges, thresholds, and limiting surfaces all defined by a precise geometry, the crypt and presbytery carry forward the significances of the past in a concentrated, bodily manner. The richness of the materials — whether it be in the grey veins of the Carrara marble floor slabs, the porous striations of the Travertine panels, the hewn and polished faces of the wooden lintel cum choir seats, or the grainy surface of the single granite stone altar — all are used to reveal nothing but the primitive and primary nature of themselves in the service of religious rituals. The corporeal here and now of each architectural element strengthens the faith in the religious institution: there is space to reflect, but no room for doubt.

O'NFD 1

O'NFD 1

Some Steps Down:
The New Crypt in Santiago's Metropolitan Cathedral, Ithaca, 2006
Rodrigo Pérez de Arce

Buried Space

A crypt usually represents the initial stage in the construction of a cathedral. At once a room and a bearer of the building's weight, it assumes the reciprocal role of origin and final destination, foundation and burial ground. In the case of the Cathedral of Santiago de Chilé, the crypt was the latest addition, thus, paradoxically becoming its only contemporary space, now lodged under the presbytery, buried and almost invisible from the nave. The new crypt's structure only secondarily contributes to the lateral reinforcement of the historical fabric, but it does not bear its weight. A project of this kind enters into sensitive rapports with its direct context. The following comments explain some of the particular characteristics of its site.

Slow fabric — Following a well established pattern, Santiago's Metropolitan Cathedral was built through a succession of reconstructions

until the outline of its general layout was found in the late 17th century. A series of interventions occurred from then until the late 19th century when its definite characteristics were consolidated through the efforts of an Italian architect driven by the firm purpose of unifying the heterogeneous parts that had been supplied by each previous incremental building phase. Even though the fake baroque figurations of this late intervention do not add significant value to the building, the designer's unifying aim was achieved. The diagrammatic strength of the rectangular box plan with its almost evenly spaced grid of piers endows the space with a quality of severe simplicity. Only minor adjustments were made to the building thereafter.

Urban matters — The building's orientation was recast in the early stages of the process: in its first layout the church flanked Santiago's main square, thus retaining a measure of autonomy from the civic — sometimes boisterous — functions of the cities prime space. Only after a process of rebuilding, which followed an earthquake, was its main axes rotated in order to preside over Santiago's prime public space that has become since then its unequivocal focus. The presence of a public garden behind its apse releases the west façade such that its silhouette acquires some urban standing. The urban setting accentuates the contrast of light and shadow between the bright — sometimes painful — exterior light and the somber interior. Subdued light, freshness, and an even, internal temperature make the building a welcome summer refuge and a relief from noise and glare.

Devotion and clutter — Like an old person's home, the Cathedral has acquired over the years a whole range of devotional elements. On the whole, these have been aligned by its side walls adhering to their fabric much like a coral reef. Each element represents the particular sensibilities of its donors. Textural richness and heterogeneous elements augment the sense of the church as a repository or a treasury. This has established an open situation such that, circumstances withstanding, the Cathedral is forever re-qualified. As for clutter, extensive railings introduced for security, severed the links between presbytery and nave, whilst also obstructing the public circulation across the apse and seriously affecting the internal uses of the church. Tall choir stalls placed behind a pavilion-like, eclectic altar added to the sense of clutter. A fake choir had blockaded the main western window.

Reciprocal layouts — Downtown Santiago is inscribed within a checkerboard pattern: Plaza de Armas, its main public place, also square in plan, is simply a missing block. The orthogonal

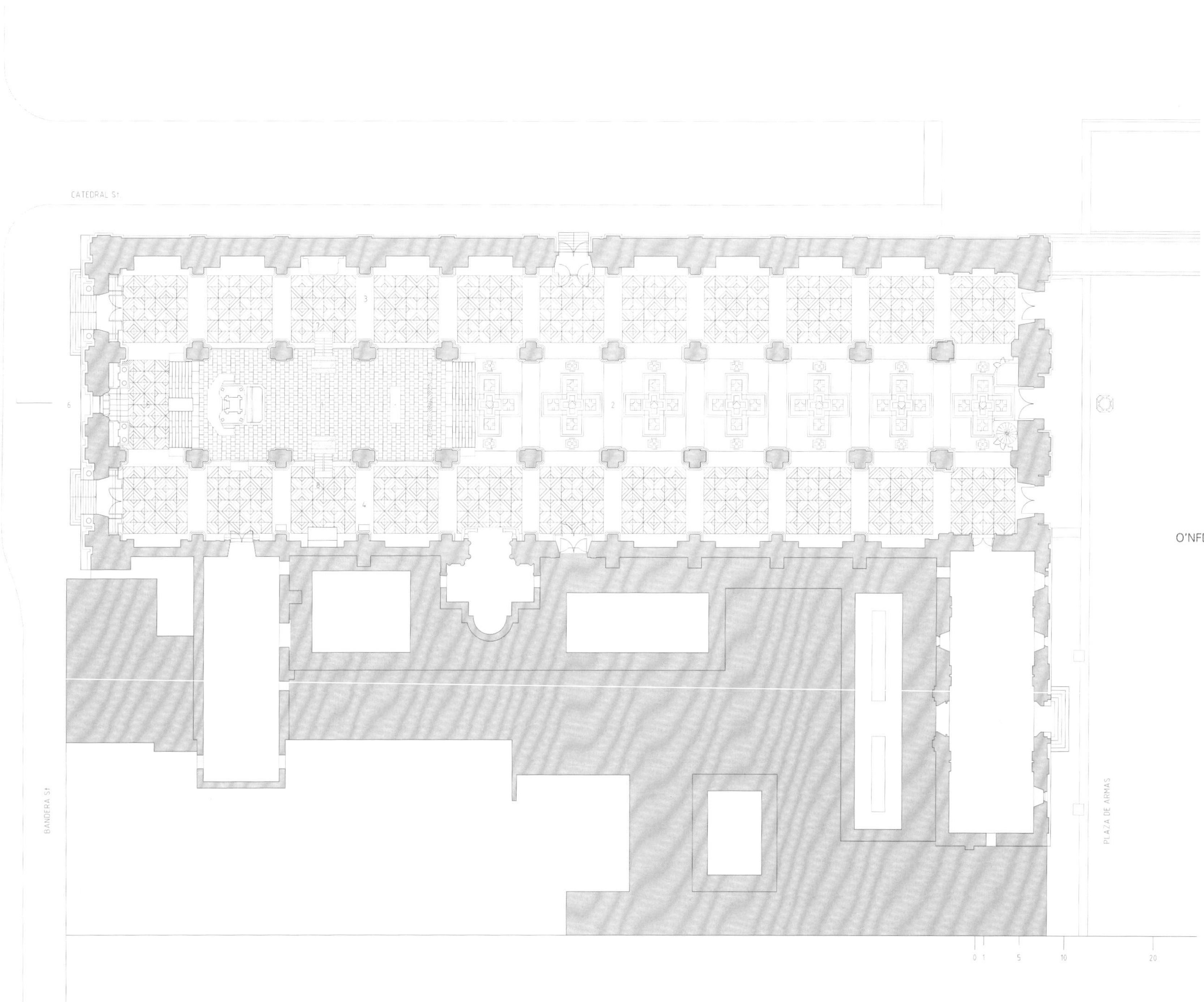

1. Presbytery, 2. Main Nave, 3. Northern Aisle, 4. Southern Aisle, 5. West Aspe,
6. Western Window , 7. Crypt Northern Entrance, 8. Crypt Southern Entrance

O'NFD 1

principle applies to all city spaces such that there is reciprocity between the urban layout and the structure of rooms. Such is also the case with the Metropolitan Cathedral and its ancillary buildings. The rectangular church plan is tightly inscribed within the square-plan urban block. An orthogonal matrix of piers is subtly inflected such that only minor differences in spans distinguish the main nave from the side aisles. This unusually neutral plan recalls the structure of a congregational mosque where all bays share equal importance. Seven doors link the nave to the surrounding spaces, such that the side aisles confronting doors in their opposite axes also become urban paths. The church is both felt and used, in certain respects, like a large covered square.

Material dimensions — Late 19th-century extensive plaster moldings and fake marble motifs characterize most of the Cathedral's interior finishes, but a recent process of restoration has resulted in the partial uncovering of the stone fabric, displaying finishes that range from the smoothest to the most coarse. As in a Brancusi sculpture, far from adding incoherence, this diversity increments the interior quality and become an engaging characteristic. The primitive and the elaborate coexist at every level. Furthermore, the subdued interior light attenuates color distinctions, while instead enhancing textural differences.

The brief — The crypt was primarily intended for the burial of archbishops and deans while also being required to serve as a memorial chapel for about 80 people. The lateral extension of the presbytery situated immediately over the crypt was later required for the purpose

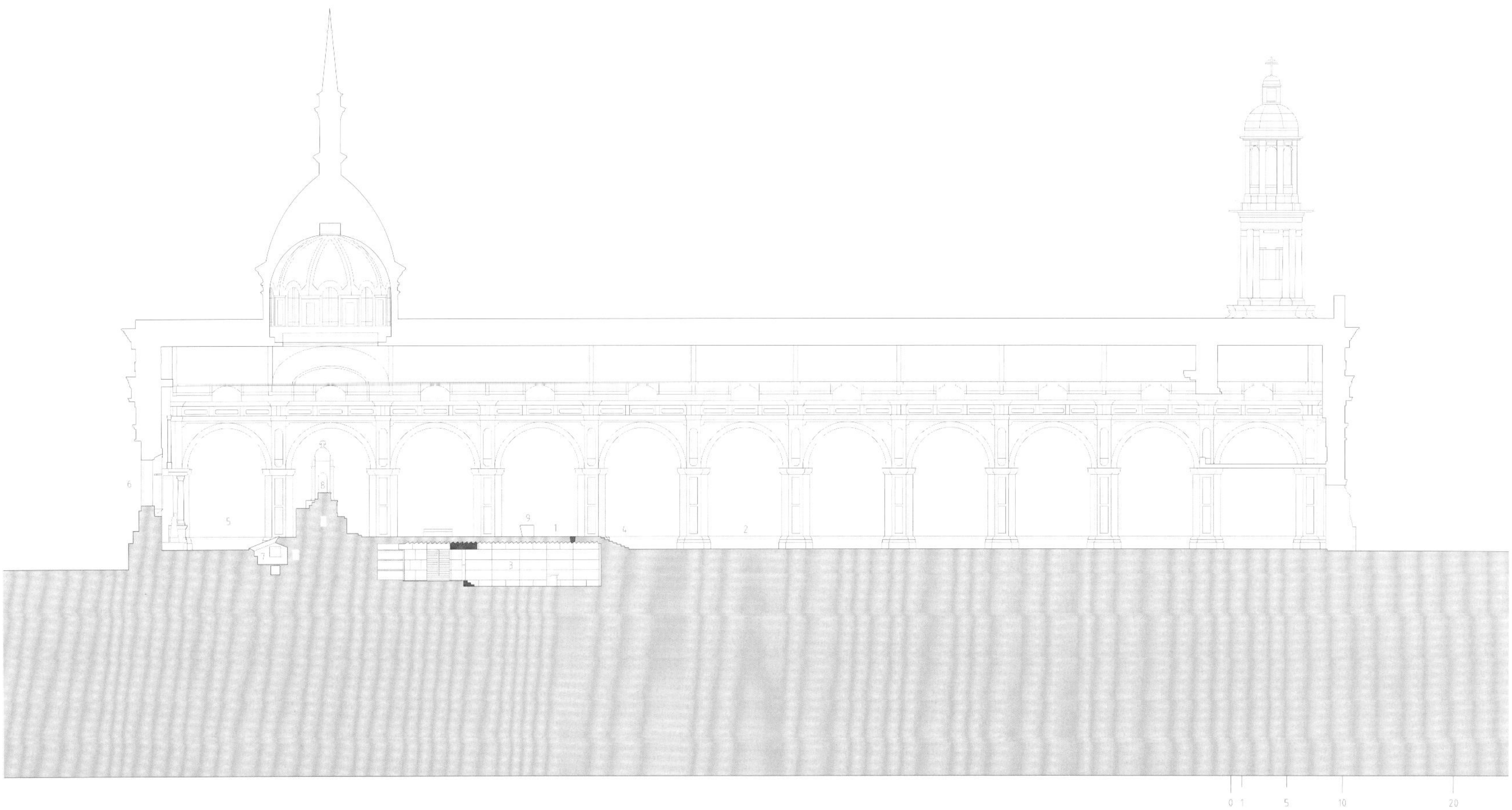

1. Presbytery
2. Main Nave
3. New Crypt
4. Eastern Steps
5. West Aspe
6. Western Window
7. Civic Crypt
8. Historic Alter
9. New Alter

of increasing its capacity to over 150 people. Also included in the client's demands were a new main altar and a small civic crypt, the latter destined to accommodate the remains of some public figures unearthed by the excavations of the presbytery. As for the quality of ambiance sought, this was defined as a serene mood, one which avoided undue insistence upon the subject of death.

The Project

The process was characterized by the extensive participation of the church authorities as well as intensive negotiations with the institution in charge of the National Monuments. Aspects of ritual, historical fidelity, and ordinary use were reviewed, together with the more intangible but equally important considerations due to the notion of character. The design principles that guided the project are described below:

To assume the openness of the process: The scheme only partially readjusts the topographic configuration of the nave, setting new processional paths and reinforcing the integration of nave and presbytery. As a result of the clearing of the apse, a new devotional setting was established that would be open to future definitions. Stone or timber inscriptions initiate an incremental process of etching into the new surfaces of the crypt.

To assume the fluid structure of circulation:
This was attained by means of aligned paths: two ranks of stairs in the presbytery (front and back) and aligned stairs to the crypt, all of them responding to processional criteria that do not admit to discontinuities or abrupt changes of direction.

To assume diversity of material finishes:
Coarse and massive timber pieces, smooth timber finishes, polished marble and basalt, coarse travertine, fair face concrete, opaque and highly polished surfaces are all present, extending the diverse language of material elaboration that characterizes the old fabric.

To subtly counteract invisibility: Inserted like a keystone in the presbytery ahead of the main altar, one massive timber beam becomes the only element that simultaneously belongs to the hidden crypt and the exposed nave. This piece also signals the position of the crypt's altar, as it supports the prime symbolic figure of a Christ. Its upper surface, set flush with the marble floor of the presbytery, is indicative of the position of the candidates to priesthood during the order-

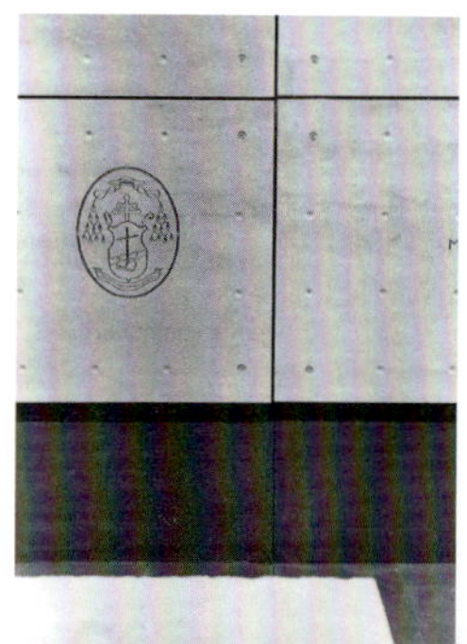

ing ceremony. Massive and slightly displaced wooden lintels, which serve a dual purpose as benches, are also indicative of the spaces underneath the presbytery.

To emphasize scale: The uncovering of the apse's historical window brings in full evening sunlight that animates the altar's background space and simultaneously highlights the full scale of the nave. The new source of light also introduces a new focus of activity.

To participate in the building's memory: The site was an archeological trove. Although in no way intending to make a comment on history, usable elements were recycled in various ways. The emphasis was formal and pragmatic. The most remarkable case was the recasting of the crypt's altar from old masonry stones.

To combine informality, intimacy, and solemnity: Heavy wooden stools will be incorporated into the small crypt, their square outline precluding preferred orientation. Only two devotional figures preside, both of Romanesque origin; these were chosen by the client and their scale intrigued us. The unusually minute ivory Pietá suggested intimate prayer as if in a private oratory within a public chapel; for this reason, it was set by the apsidal wall and at eye-height.

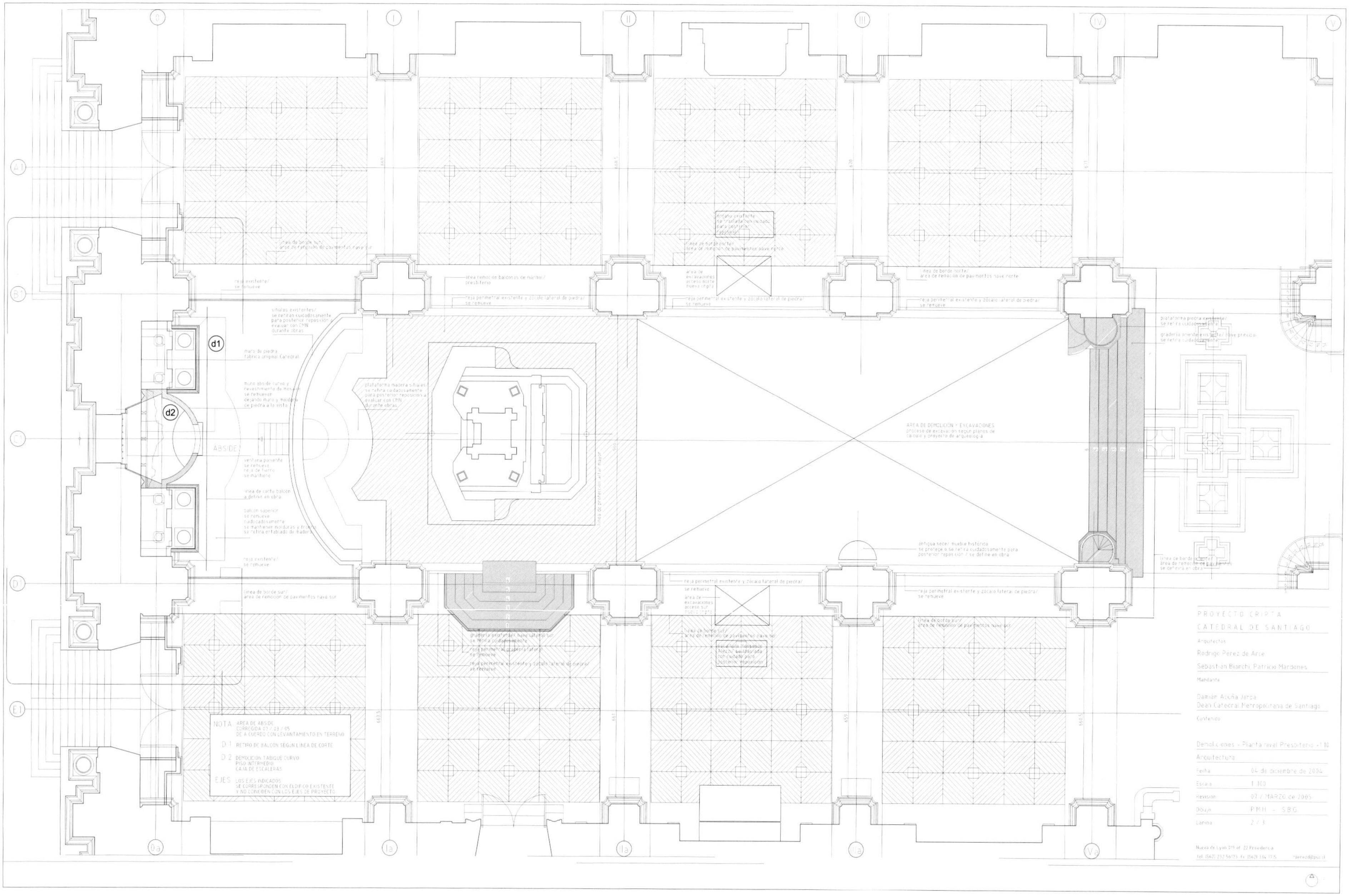

NOTA AREA DE ABSIDE
CORREGIDA 07 / 03 / 05
DE A CUERDO CON LEVANTAMIENTO EN TERRENO
D 1 RETIRO DE BALCON SEGUN LINEA DE CORTE
D 2 DEMOLICION TABIQUE CURVO
PISO INTERMEDIO
CAJA DE ESCALERAS
EJES LOS EJES INDICADOS
SE CORRESPONDEN CON ELDIFICO EXISTENTE
Y NO COINCIDEN CON LOS EJES DE PROYECTO
ABSIDE
PROYECTO CRIPTA
CATEDRAL DE SANTIAGO
Arquitectos
Rodrigo Pérez de Arce
Sebastián Bianchi, Patricio Mardones
Mandante
Damián Acuña Jarpa
Dean Catedral Metropolitana de Santiago
Contenido
Demoliciones - Planta nivel Presbiterio +1.10
Arquitectura
Fecha 04 de diciembre de 2004
Escala 1:100
Revision 07 / MARZO de 2005
Dibujo PMH - SBG
Lamina 2 / 3
Nueva de Lyon 019 of. 22 Providencia

To emphasize the descending access: Burial is about returning to the ground: its path is always downward. Two massive timber lintels mark the place of access to the underground. The material of the steps changes from marble to timber, provoking distinctive differences in sonority within the descent to the crypt. The underground space is also divided topographically to create a sort of atrium that acts as a preamble to the chapel. A heavy lintel and a set of sliding fences indicate the threshold to the underground chapel. As in an Escher composition the same configurations of steps characterize the approach stairs, the fair faced concrete ceiling, and the apsidal wall. Besides providing textural richness these configurations improve the internal acoustics.

The homogenous white marble surface of the presbytery floor contributes to a luminous ambiance within the twilight atmosphere of the nave. It seemed appropriate to keep lighting levels subtle given the harshness of the natural light in Santiago, maintaining thus the quality of the nave as a cool and restful public setting.

PROYECTO CRIPTA
CATEDRAL DE SANTIAGO
Arquitectos
Rodrigo Perez de Arce
Sebastián Bianchi, Patricio Mardones
Mandante
Damián Acuña Jarpa
Dean Catedral Metropolitana de Santiago
Contenido
Demoliciones – Corte longitudinal
Arquitectura
Fecha: 04 de diciembre de 2004
Escala 1:100
Revisión 07 / Marzo de 2005
Dibujo PMH – SBG
Lámina 1 / 3
ABSIDE
CRIPTA EXISTENTE
ALTAR MAYOR HISTÓRICO
ÁREA NUEVA CRIPTA
nuevas gradas presbiterio
+- 0.0 nivel nave principal
gradas presbiterio existentes/
se remueven
Nota: Las plantas consideran el
desfase entre los ejes
norte-sur, correspondientes a
los pilares de la nave central.
Todas las medidas se verificarán
en obra

d1
d2
d2

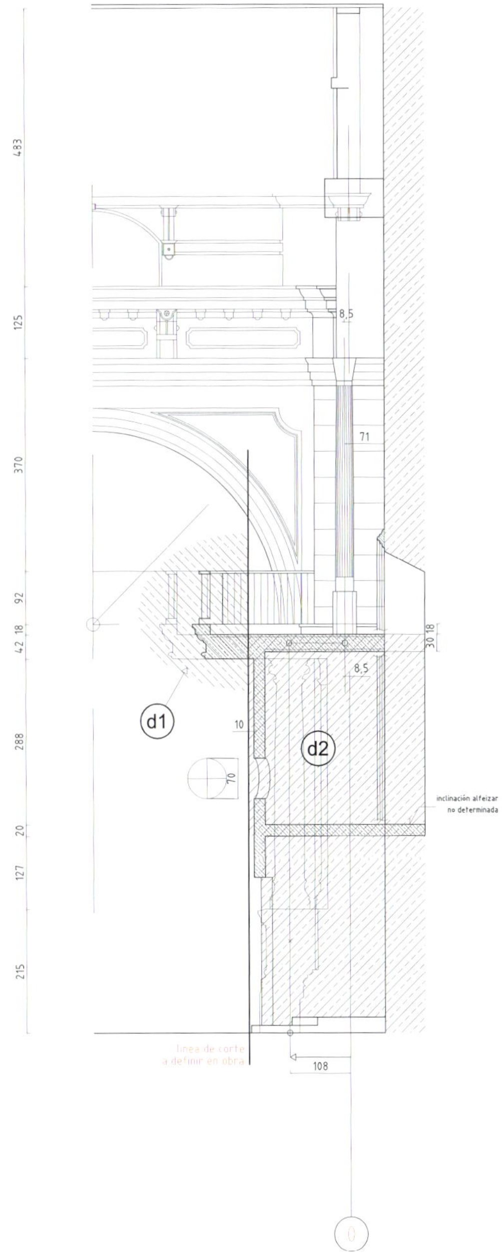
483
125
370
92
42 18
288
20
127
215
8,5
71
30 18
8,5
10
70
d1
d2
inclinación alfeizar
no determinada
línea de corte
a definir en obra
108

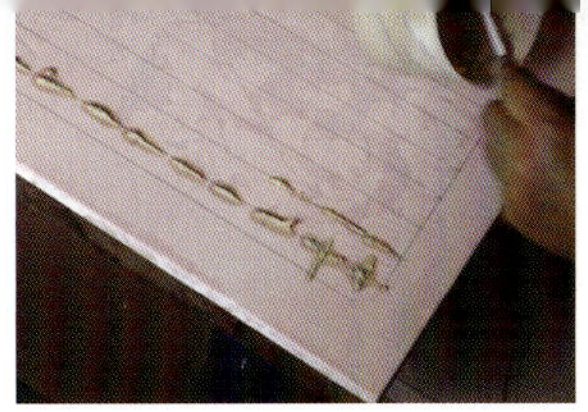

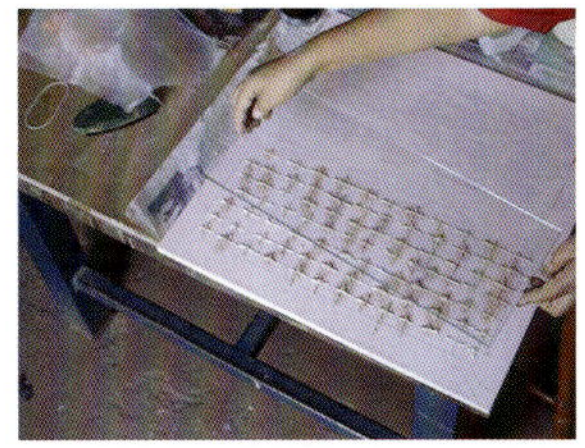

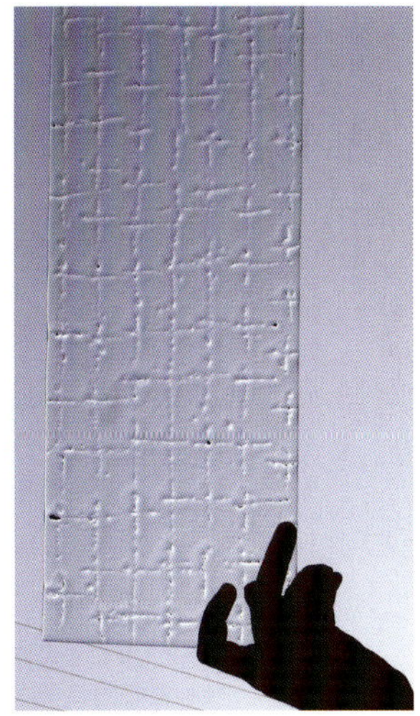

DIEGO PORTALES PALAZUELOS
1793
1837
AMÓ Y SIRVIÓ A LA PATRIA

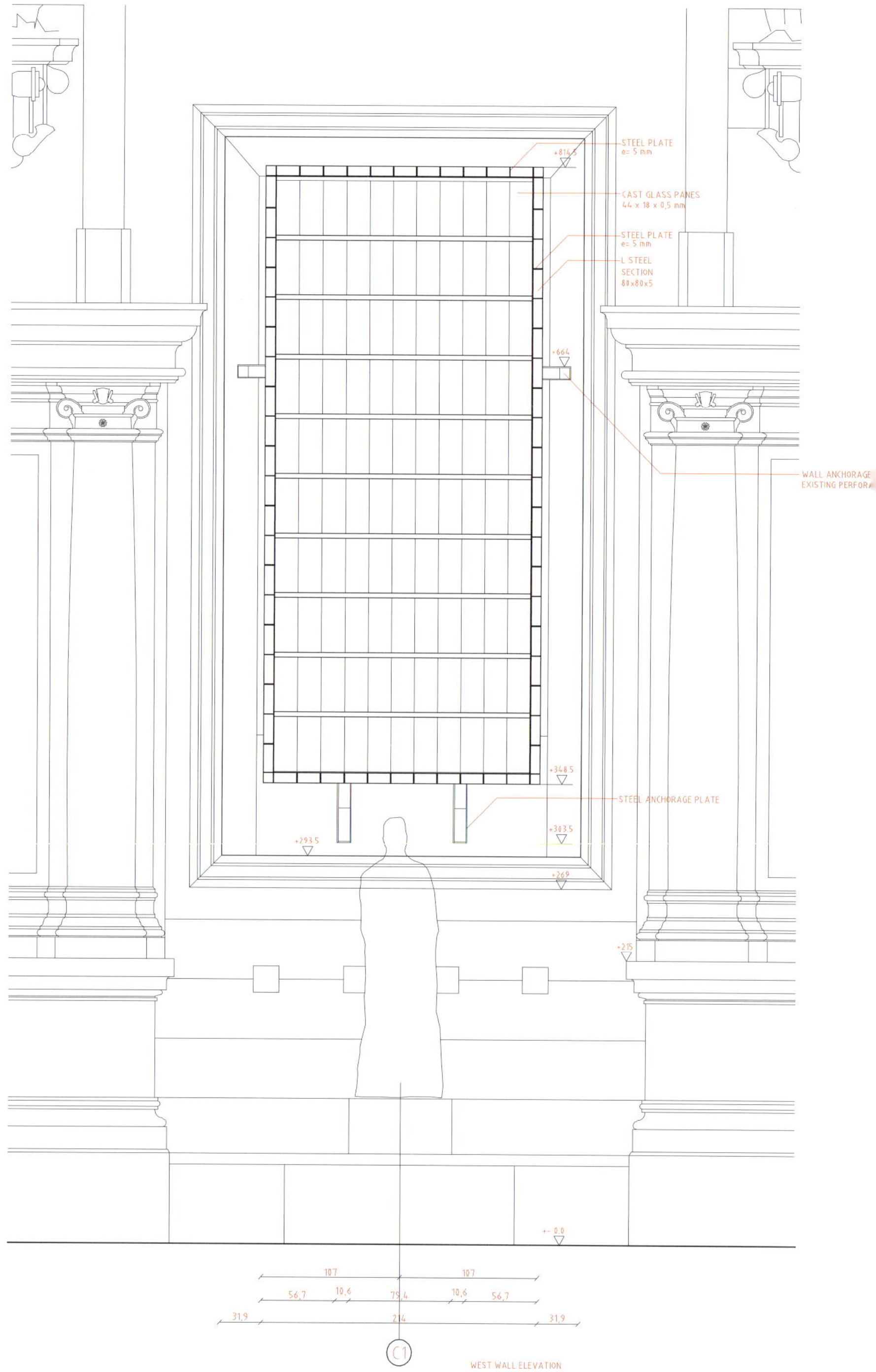
STEEL PLATE
e= 5 mm
+814.5
CAST GLASS PANES
44 x 18 x 0,5 mm
STEEL PLATE
e= 5 mm
L STEEL
SECTION
80x80x5
+664
WALL ANCHORAGE
+348.5
STEEL ANCHORAGE PLATE
+303.5
+293.5
+269
+215
+- 0.0
107
107
56,7
10,6
79,4
10,6
56,7
31,9
214
31,9
C1
WEST WALL ELEVATION

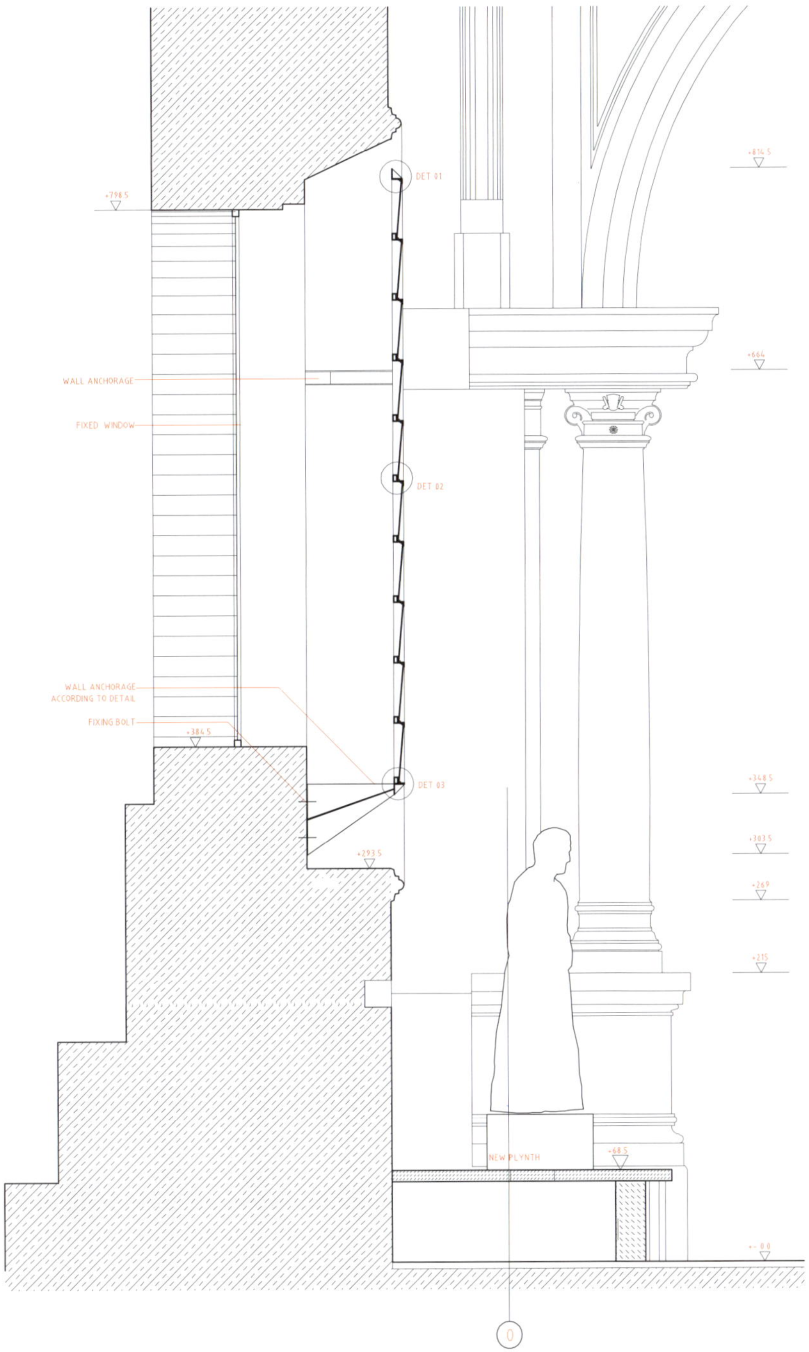

WEST WALL SECTION

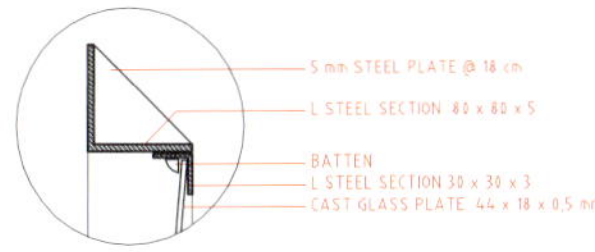

DETAIL 01

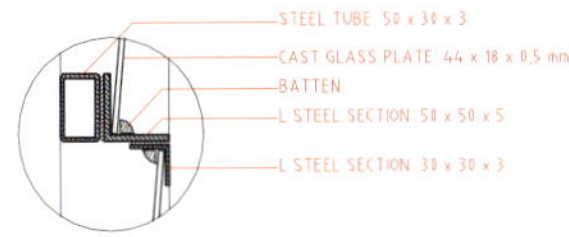

DETAIL 02

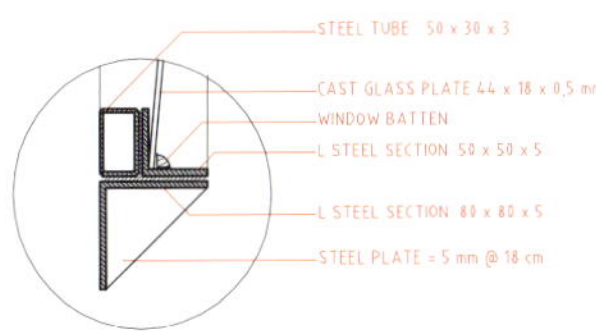

DETAIL 03

Blocked by a series of accretions the western window was out of sight for many years. Consequently, the apse was a somber and uninviting space. A prime intention of the project was to restore the original light conditions of the nave through the removal of the invasive structures, thus reincorporating the apse into the traditional ambulatory path. The heavily textured glazed screen tiles attenuate the harsh western light.

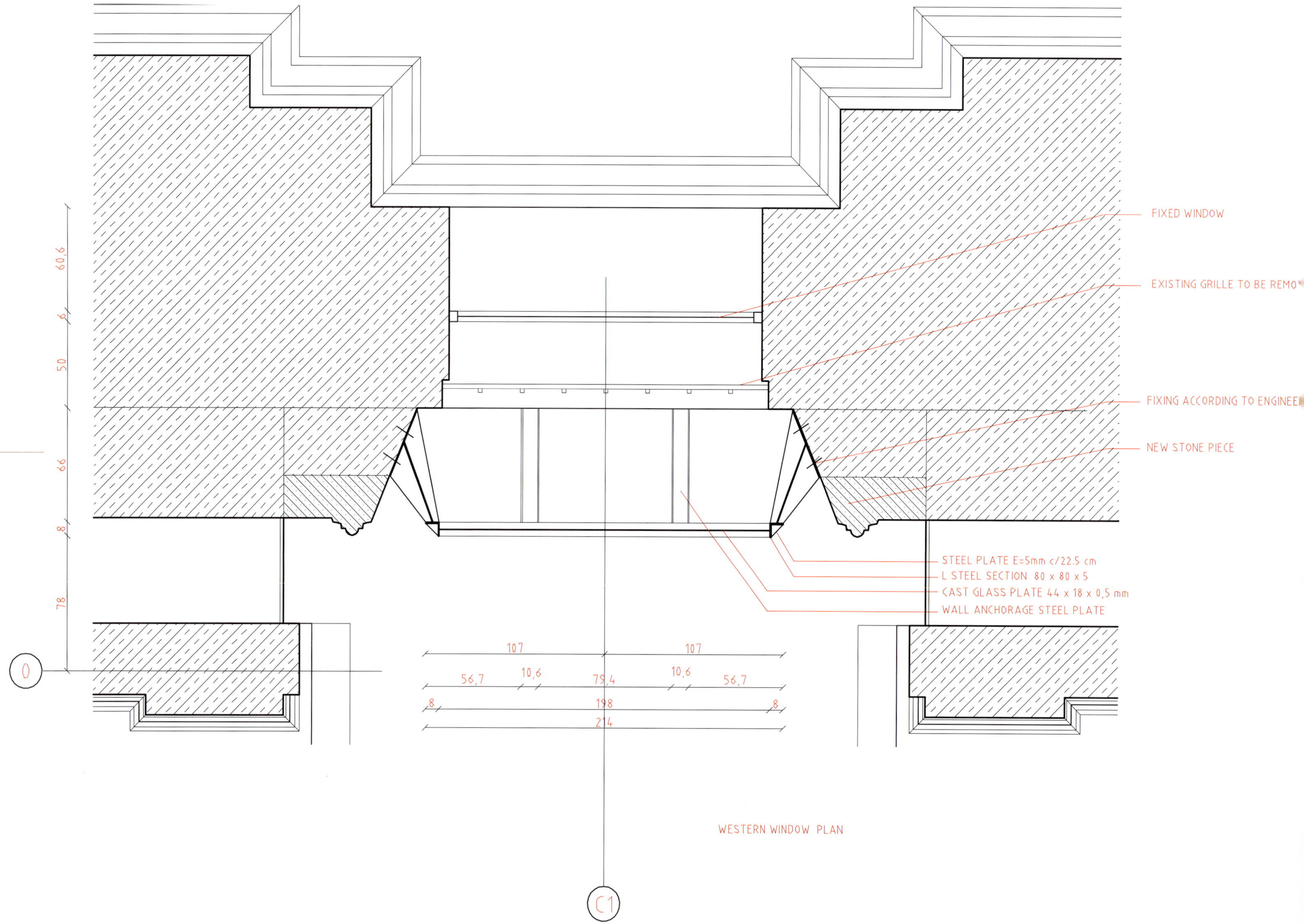

WESTERN WINDOW PLAN

A small crypt was accommodated toward the Cathedral apse, in order to receive the remains of statesmen formerly buried under the presbytery whose coffins were unearthed during the archaeological digs. Laid upon it following the incline of the rank of steps, the marble slab reflects the western light.

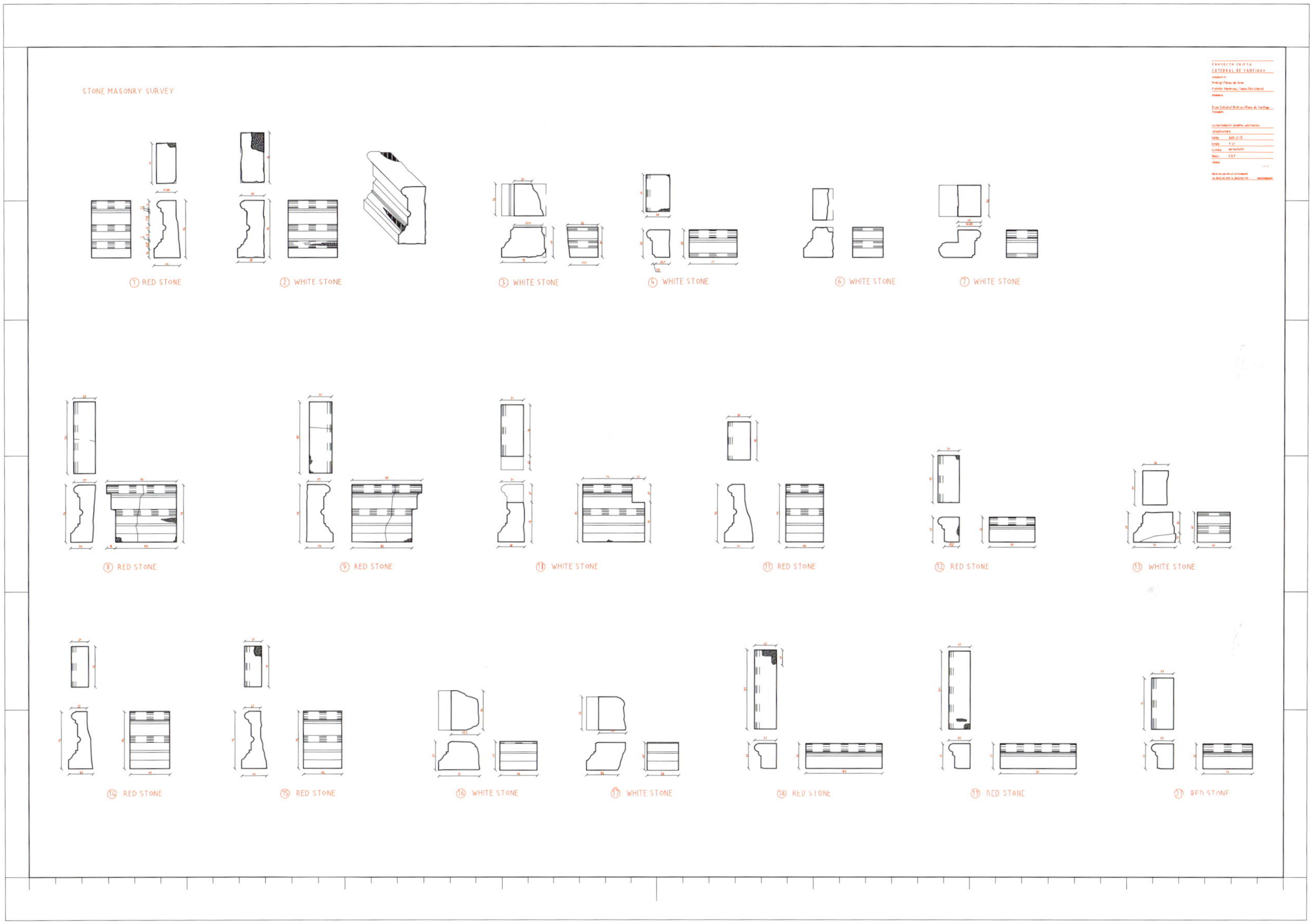

An extensive archaeological search was realized as a prelude to the construction of the crypt. Prime historical pieces such as stone foundations were removed for preservation while most of the masonry stone pieces recovered from the old presbytery were recycled within the new scheme.

A seemingly solid granite altar sculpted by Marcela Correa commands the renovated presbytery. As agreed with the clients, the massive piece follows the ancient model of the sacrificial stone as opposed to the idea of the altar as a gathering table. The monolithic piece was carved from a quarry situated in the nearby Andean mountain range. The piece was internally emptied to remove from the granite block enough weight as required by the supporting structure's bearing capacity.

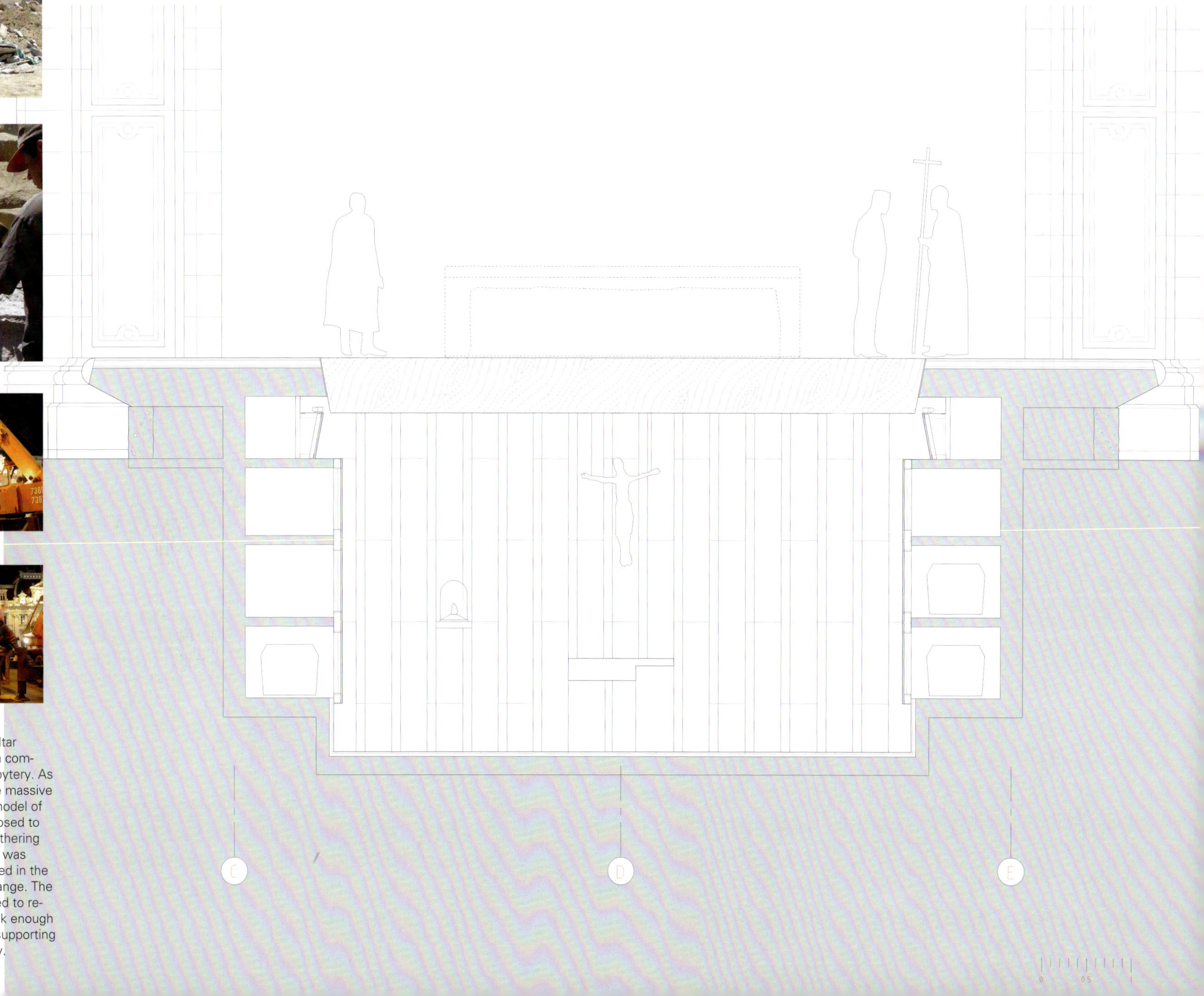

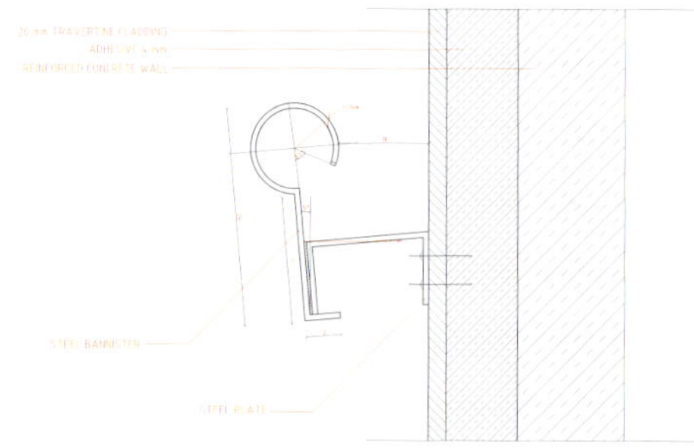

O'NFD 1

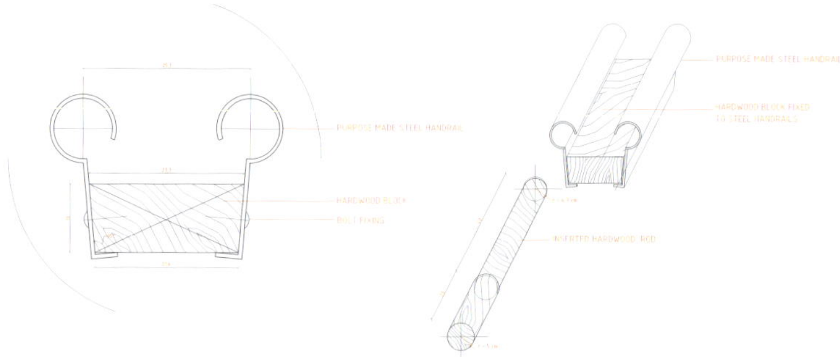

The issue with handrails was how to provide support and protection while being as silent and unobtrusive as possible in relation to the side aisles. It was intended that the insertion of the new crypt within the body of the church be discreet. Carrara marble slabs and the flying handrails are the only elements beyond the confinement of the renovated presbytery projecting into the aisles.

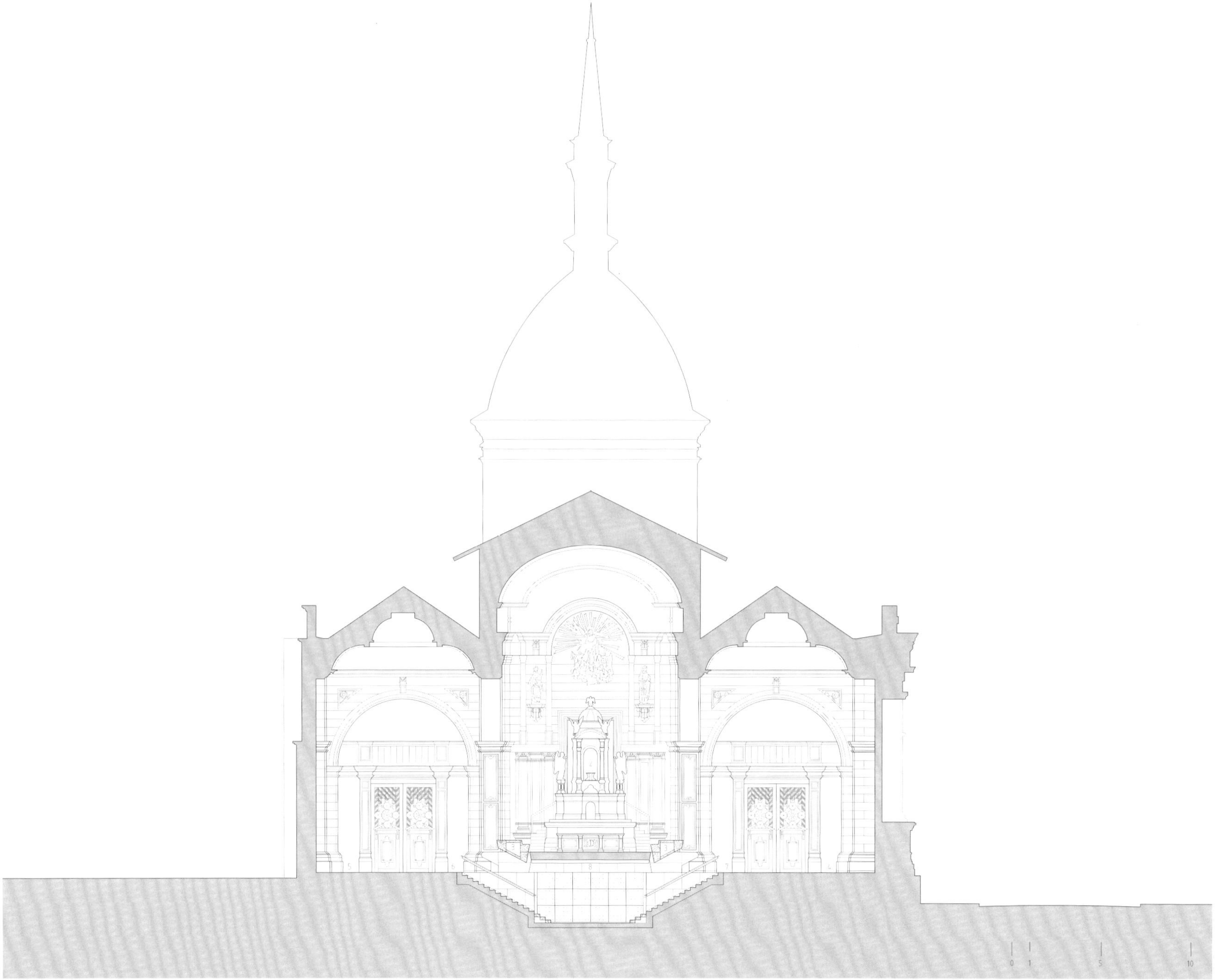

1. Presbytery, 2. Historical Altar, 3. Wooden Lintels, 4. Northern Aisle, 5. Southern Aisle,
6. Crypt Southern Entrance, 7. Crypt Northern Entrance, 8. Atrium

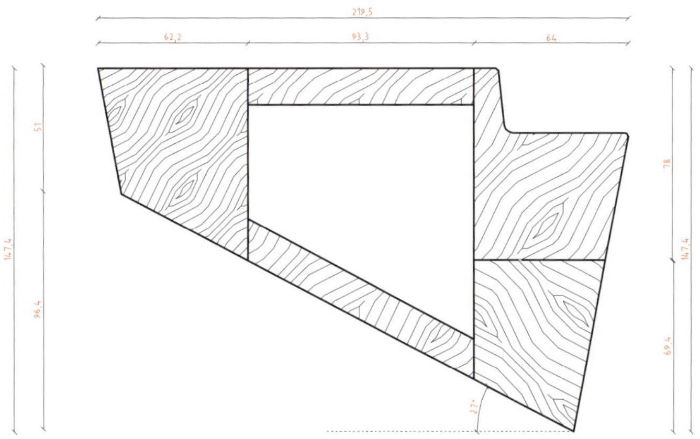
219,5
62,2
93,3
64
51
147,4
96,4
78
147,4
69,4
27°

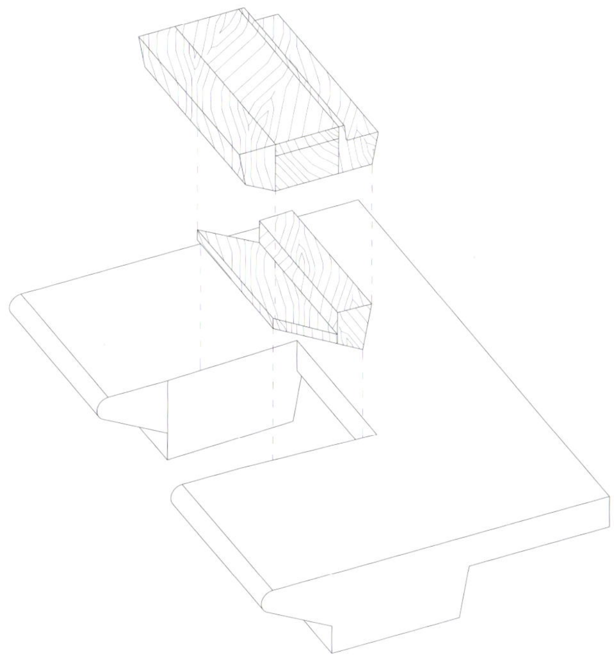

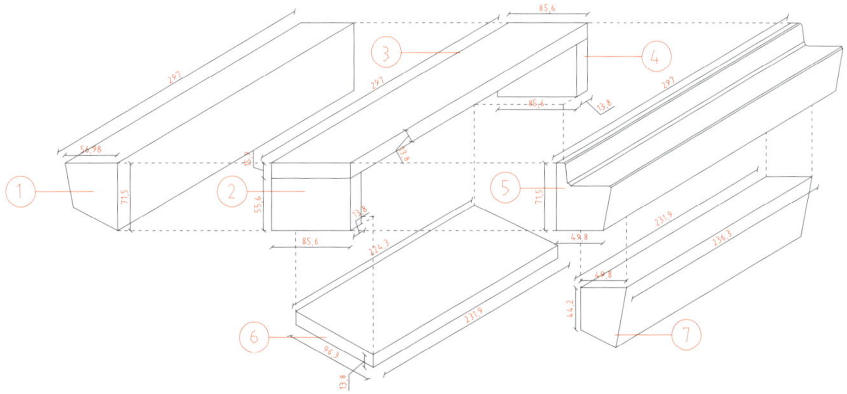
1
2
3
4
5
6
7
297
85,6
71,5
55,6
13,8
224,3
231,9
236,3
49,8
44,2
96,3

DEL POZO Y SILVA
1745
Con el Hijo en tu regazo,
como en Belén y el Calvario,
Virgen de la Piedad óyenos,
guíanos hacia la casa
donde el Padre nos aguarda.
Amén.

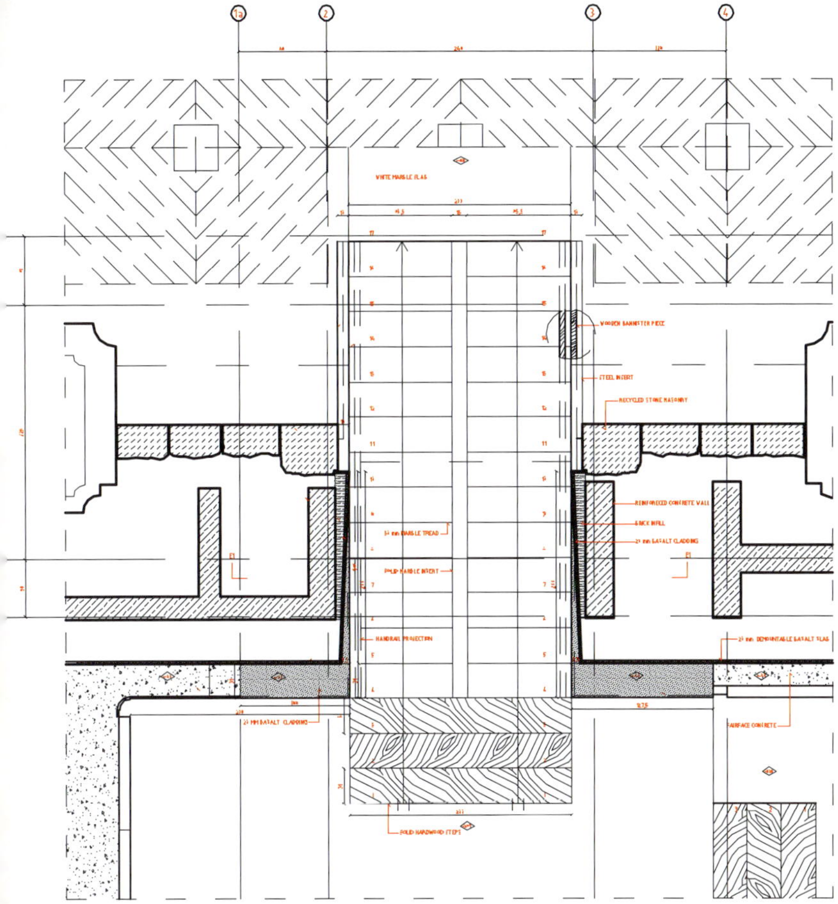

CRYPT ACCES STAIRS PLAN AT [illegible] LEVEL.

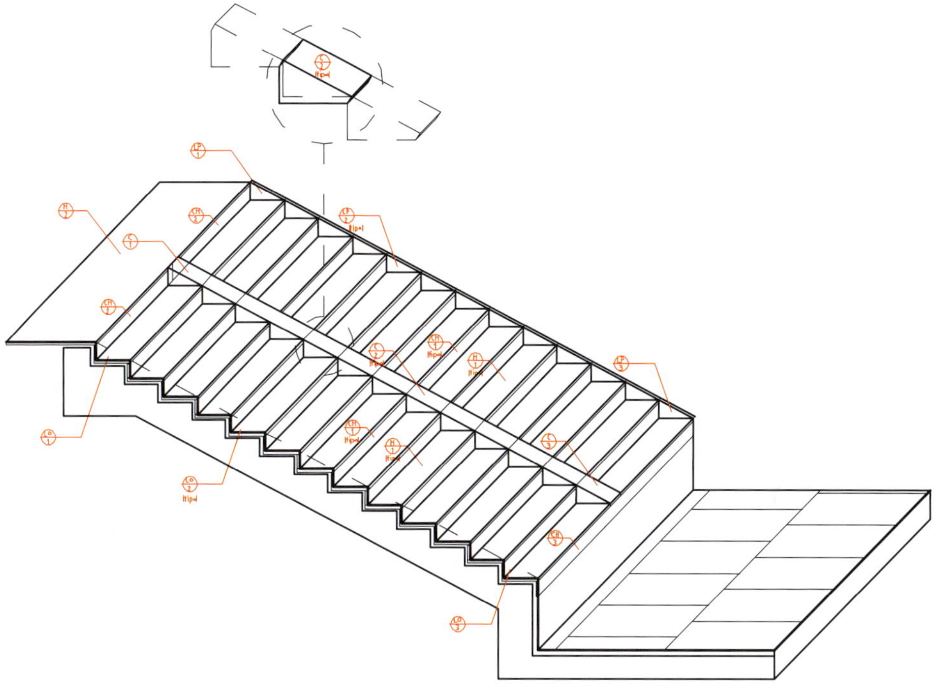

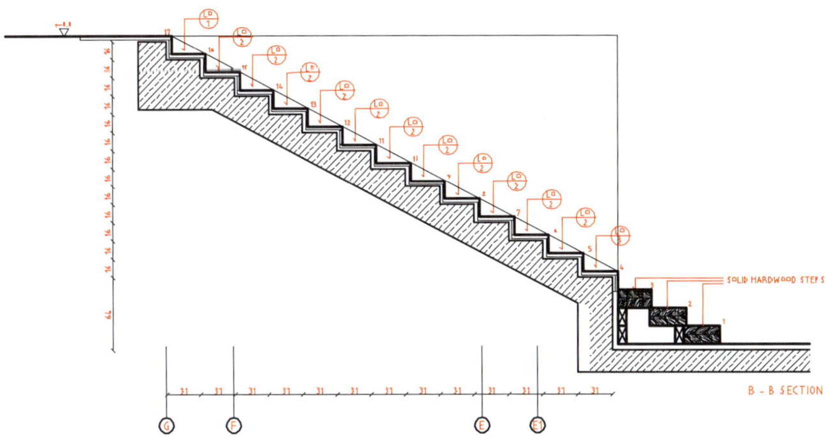

B - B SECTION

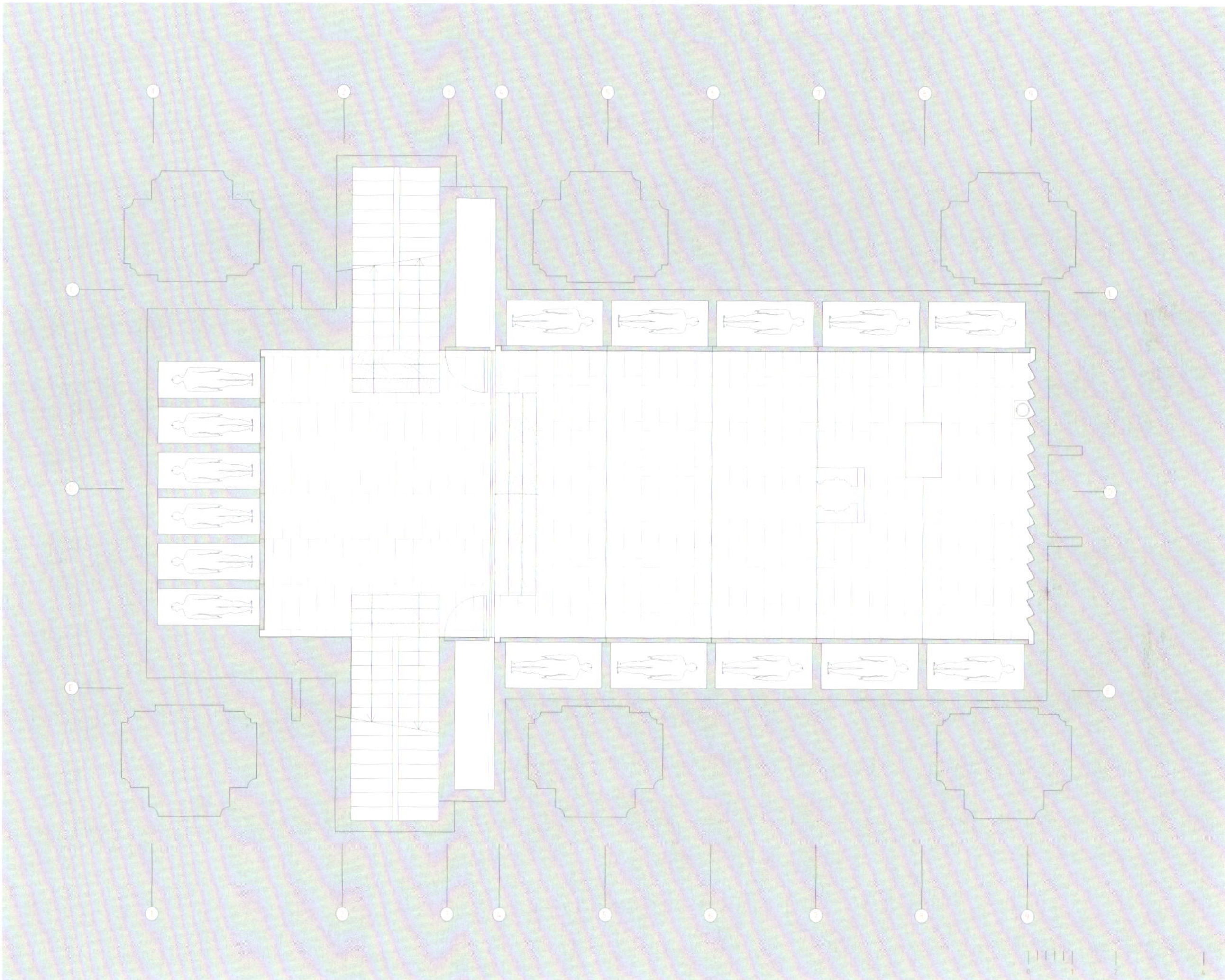

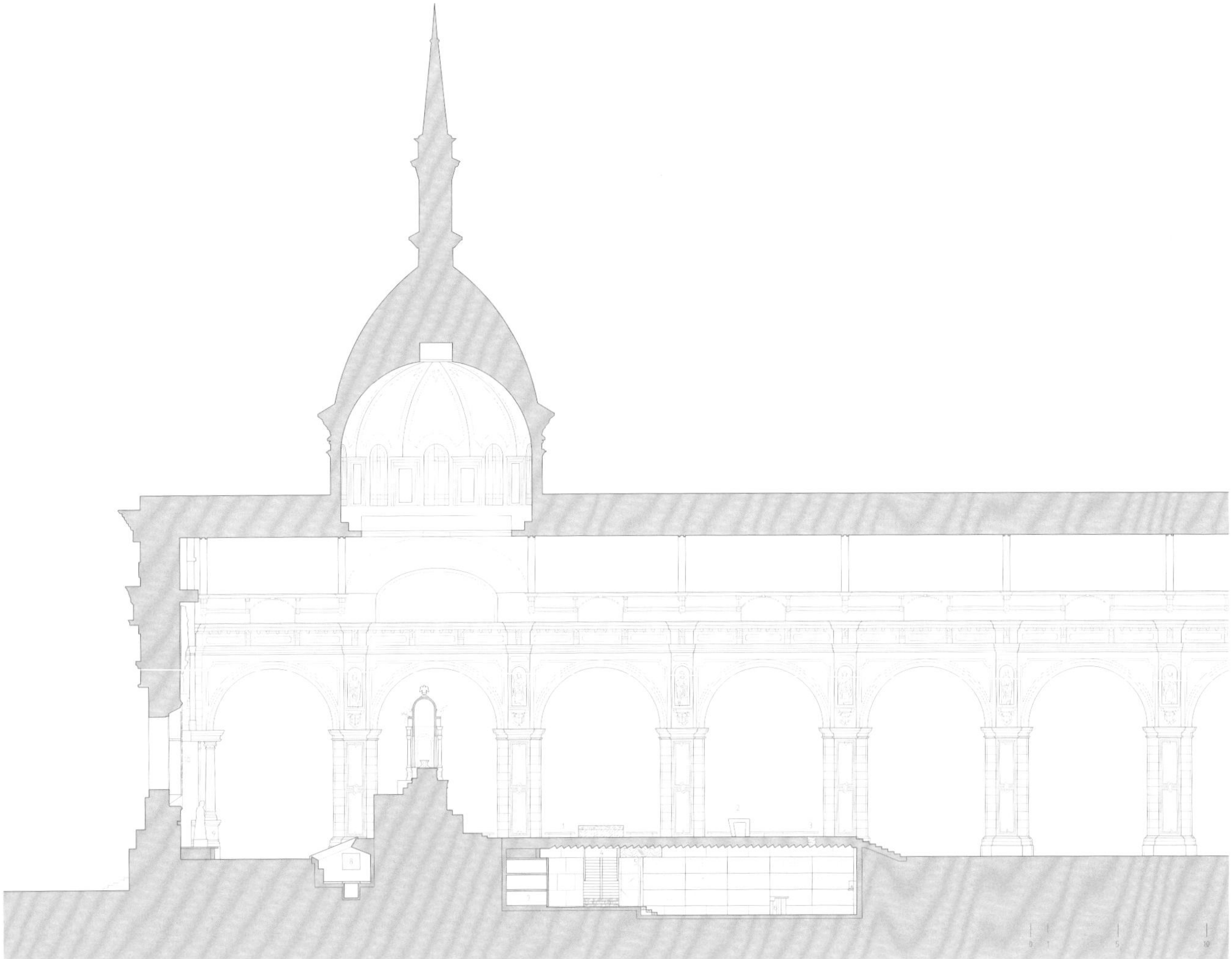

1. Presbytery, 2. New Alter, 3. Inserted Timber Beam, 4. Crypt Northern Entrance, 5. Wooden Lintel,
6. Crypt Altar, 7. Deans Tombs, 8. Civic Crypt, 9. New Devotional Setting, 10. Ornamental Glass Tiles

CARDENAL CARLOS OVIEDO CAVADA
MONSEÑOR MARIANO CASANOVA CASANO

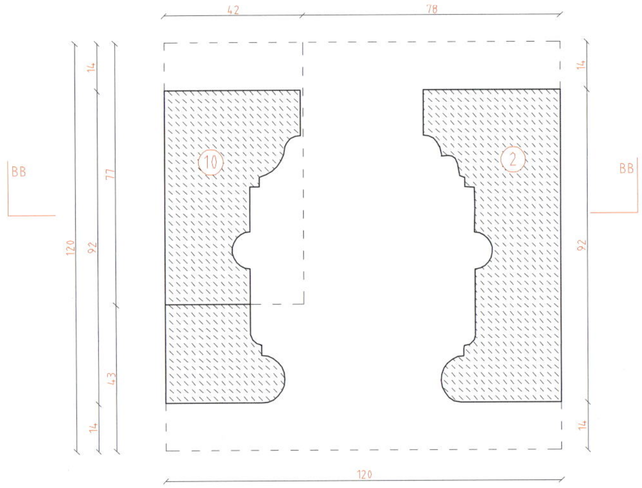

ALTAR PLAN

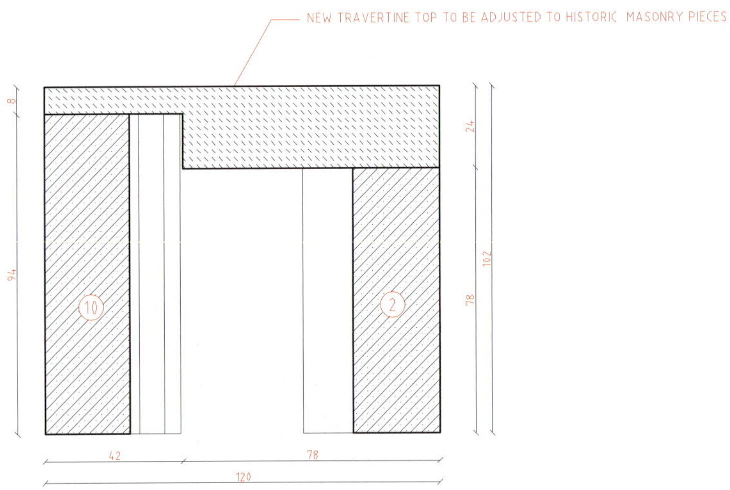

BB SECTION

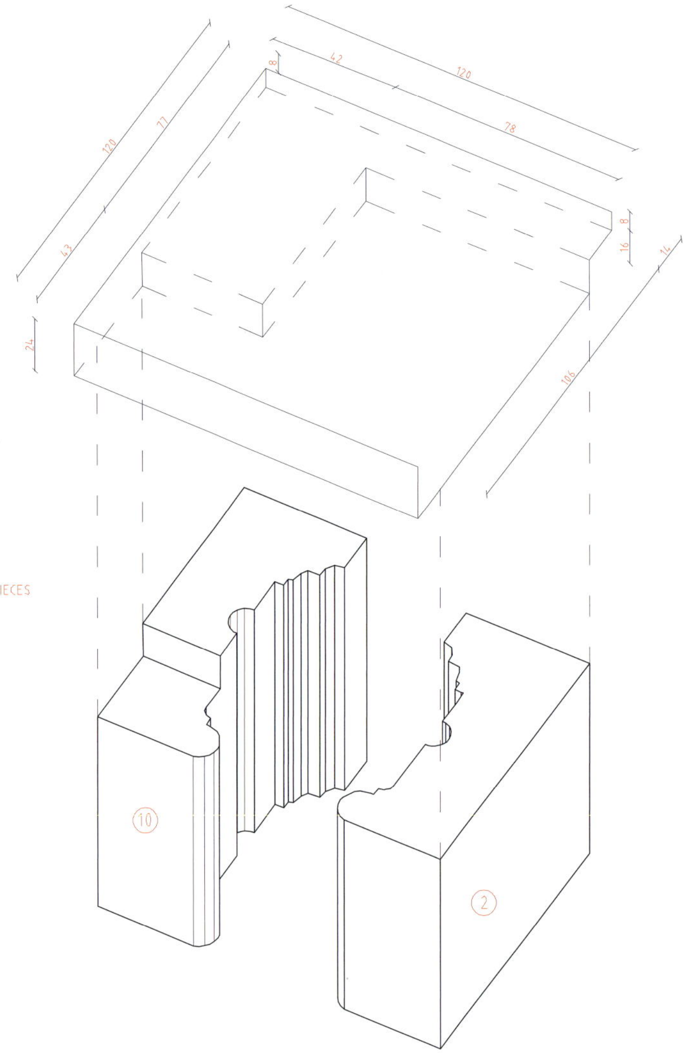

Two recycled bases and a new travertine top comprise the robust figure of the altar. Its square plan ameliorates the formal effect of its strict axial emplacement. Much like a curtain, the travertine folded wall, its profile identical to that of the concrete slab, covers the back of the Chapel and counteracts reverberation. Resting upon a small ledge stands a tiny, 14th-century, Romanesque ivory figure of a Pieta originally made as a response to the Black Plague that devastated Europe. Its intimate scale is unusual for a public setting: located at eye level it invites private prayer.

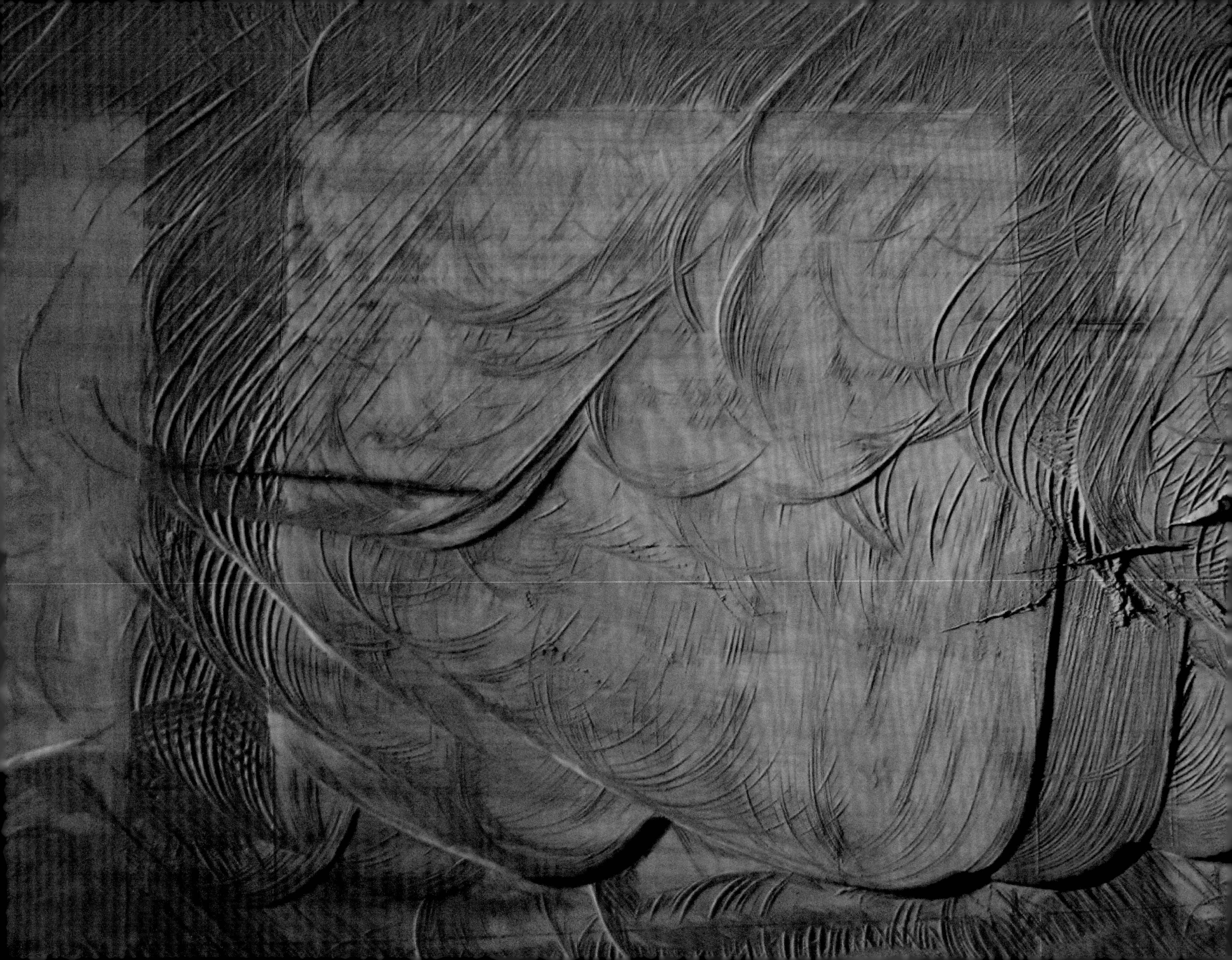

As with a Brancusi sculpture, material finishes within the nave are extremely diverse. The saw-mill cuts made into the heavy native Oak timbers are left exposed in affinity with the material roughness that characterizes some of the Cathedral's finishes. These massive pieces, doubling up as lintels, choir seats and plinths, rest upon the smooth presbytery floor.

DEAN JUAN PÉREZ GUZMÁN
DEAN JUAN PÉREZ GUZMÁN

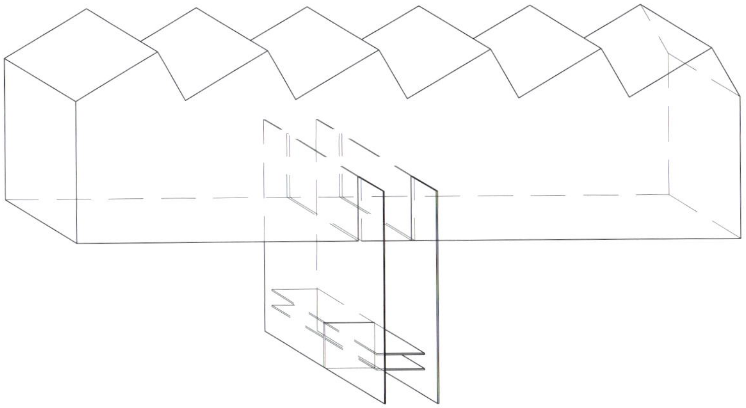

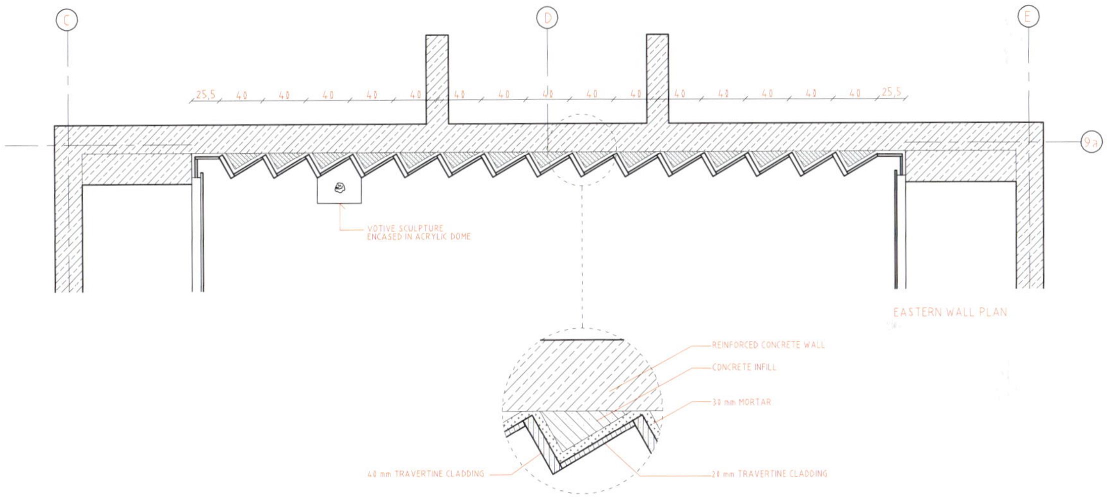

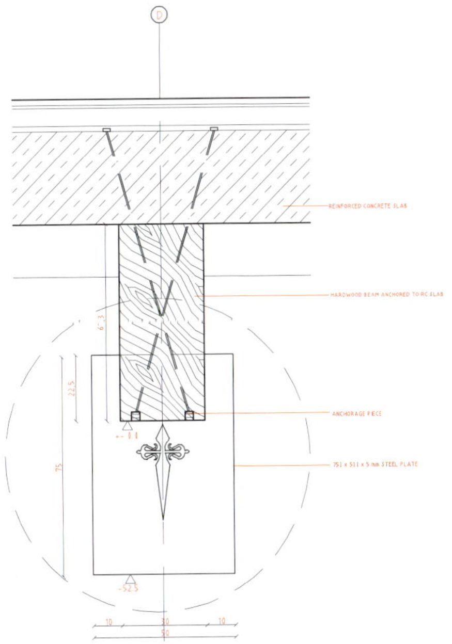

Firmly locked into the concrete slab, an oak beam indicates the threshold into the crypt acting also as and mediating device between ceiling and sliding doors. The beam embodies the rotating movement of the public upon entry into the chapel. The massive oak beam from which hangs the Romanesque figure of the Christ is loosely associated with the idea of the cross. Its soffit profile exactly follows the concrete slab relief pattern, so that its presence is only perceived within close range.

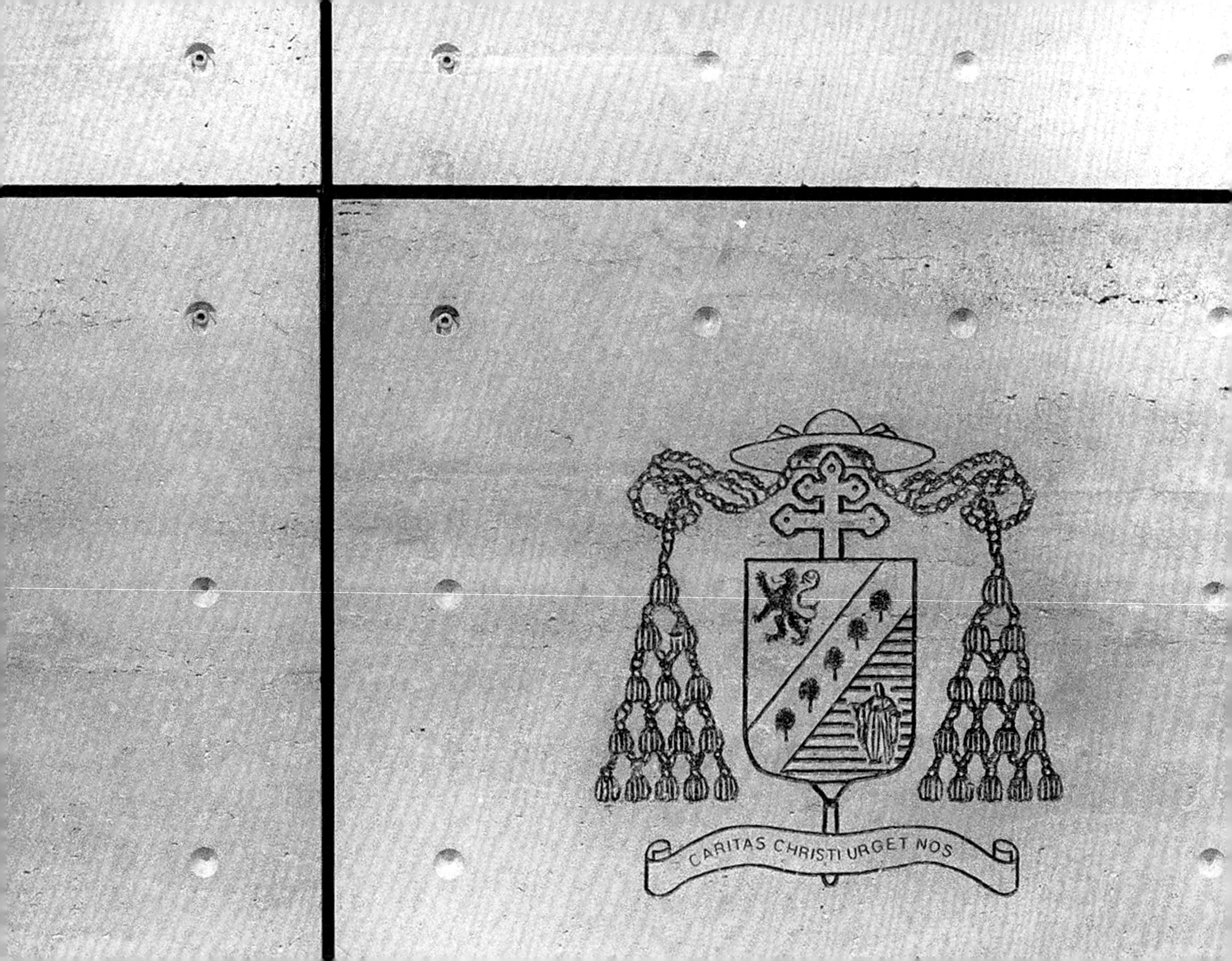
CARITAS CHRISTI URGET NOS

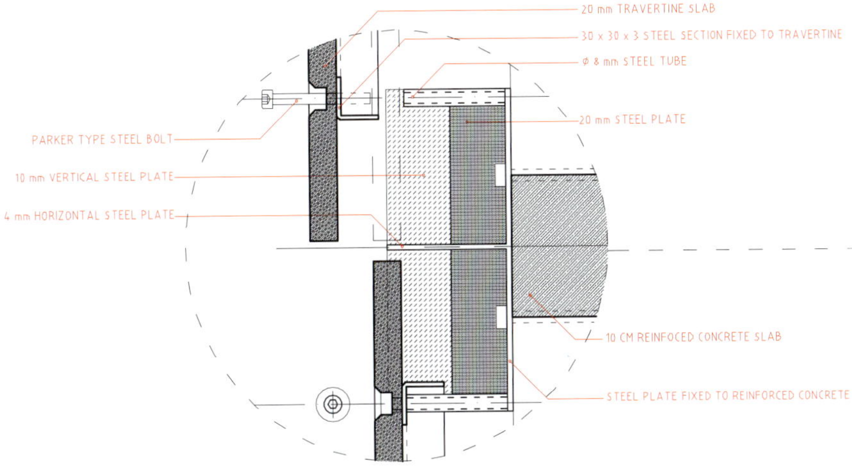

TYPICAL FIXING DETAIL esc. 1:2

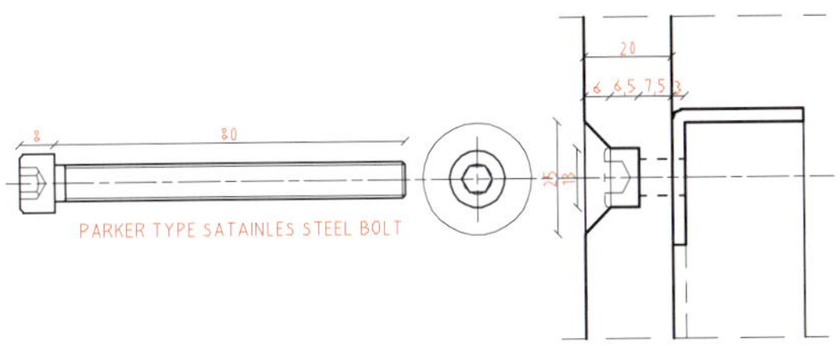

ANCHORAGE DETAIL

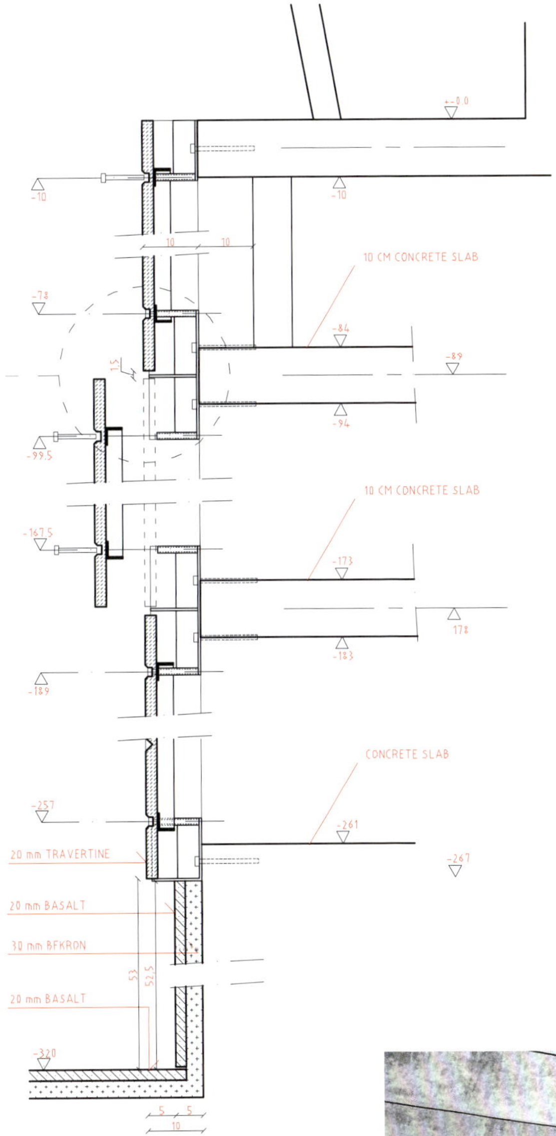

Following tradition, personal emblems signal each bishop's burial place. The graphic design project considered a faithful transcription of the hand-carved figures which belonged to the original tombstones into the travertine slabs. These original pieces loosely followed pattern-book graphics.

March 9, 10, 11, 2005. Octagonal small room within square-shaped masonry and lime structure (5,8 m x 5,8 m).

This piece was the Capilla Real foundation; once the first built stage of Santiago's new Cathedral was opened in 1775, it was the place arranged for civil authorities to attend religious services. Several interventions are noticeable within the structure; many of them were probably implemented by Italian architect Joaquín Toesca in 1789, who adapted it as King Carlos III cenotaph foundation during the celebration of his funeral rites.

The masonry block appeared at the beginning of the fourth layer of the archeological excavation (20 cm depth). Its walls are 80 cm high, and its foundation goes down 170 cm.

May 19, 2005. Remains of the family seat formerly placed in Santiago´s Cathedral site bought by the Church in 1748.

A bricked floor room was found at this excavation layer (between 203 and 330 cm depth). It had two openings (one oriented to the Northwest, another corresponding to a door) and a stone buttress describing a small hallway. The door leads to an exterior courtyard paved with pebbled geometric patterns; at North it borders on the prolongation of the room's adobe wall. To the Southwest there is a corridor delimited with ashlar blocks (the same as used for wall foundations) that suggests the passageway outlined for accessing other rooms.

Other features with same characteristics were found in other adjacent areas of this colonial layer. Thus, it is possible to assume a certain idea of the whole house and its major configuration, which fits other documented descriptions from that period.

Appendices

Biographies

House at Punta Pite

Smiljan Radic Clarke graduated from the Universidad Católica de Chilé and thereafter studied at the Istituto Universitario di Architettura di Venezia, Italy. He has worked in Iraklio, Greece in association with the architects Nikolas Skutelis and Flavio Zanon and in 2001 was recognized as the best national architect less than 35 years old by the Chiléan Architects Association. He continues to work in Santiago, often in collaboration with the sculptor Marcela Correa.

Crypt in the Cathedral of Santiago de Chilé

Rodrigo Pérez de Arce is a tenured professor at the Catholic University School of Architecture in Santiago from where he graduated. He has taught at various schools, including the Architectural Association in London and the University of Cornell in Ithaca, and has lectured extensively in Europe and the United States. Currently, he is Visiting Critic at the University of East London. He has realized many public projects in association with other architects, such as the Mapocho Cultural Centre and the Renovation of Santiago's main Square, and he has received numerous design and publication awards including commendation from the Mies Van der Rohe Foundation for Plaza de Armas and the Carlos Raul Villanueva Essay Prize.

Sebastián Bianchi Gajardo is Professor of Architecture at the Universidad Nacional Andrés Bello and the Pontificia Universidad Católica in Santiago, Chilé, where he received both his bachelor and masters degrees in Architecture. Both independently, and as associate to Rodrigo Pérez de Arce, his professional practice has received several design awards and has been published both nationally and internationally. At present he is working on curating and producing the retrospective exhibition entitled The Architecture, Process and Paintings of Guillaume Jullian de la Fuente.

Patricio Mardones graduated from the Pontificia Universidad Católica de Chilé in 1999 and has worked in various architecture offices since 1997. Since 2001, he has worked in association with Rodrigo Pérez de Arce, and with Cecilia Puga since 2003. Mardones has taught in project design studios at the Schools of Architecture at the Pontificia Universidad Católica de Chilé (2001-2006), the Universidad Diego Portales (2002-2005), and the Universidad Andrés Bello in Santiago (2005-2006), where he is a full professor. He was a Visiting Professor at The University of Texas, Austin in 2007. Mardones has published numerous articles in international magazines and is currently Editorial Assistant Director of Ediciones ARQ produced by the Pontificia Universidad Católica de Chilé School of Architecture.

Editors

Kevin Alter is the Academic Director for Architecture Programs, Associate Dean for Graduate Programs, Sid W. Richardson Centennial Professor of Architecture, Director of the Summer Academy in Architecture, and Associate Director of the Center for American Architecture and Design at The University of Texas at Austin. He is a graduate of Bennington College and of Harvard University. His professional practice, alterstudio architects, has received several design awards and has been published both nationally and internationally. Alter has edited several books published by the Center and his writing has also appeared in various architectural publications. He has curated many exhibitions, including Building the California Dream: The Eichler Homes; Conception and Construction: Five Swiss Architects; and The Work of Alvaro Siza, all of which have appeared in numerous international venues.

Wilfried Wang is the O'Neil Ford Centennial Professor in Architecture at The University of Texas at Austin. Together with Barbara Hoidn, Wang established the office of Hoidn Wang Partner in Berlin in 2001. He studied architecture in London, where he was in partnership with John Southall. In 1979, he was founding Co-Editor of 9H Magazine and Co-Director of the 9H Gallery from 1985 to 1990. From 1995 to 2000 he was director of the German Architecture Museum. He has taught at the Polytechnic of North London, University College London, ETH Zurich, Harvard University, and University of Navarra and has also authored numerous architectural publications and served on various competition and award juries. He is an honorary member of the Federation of German Architects and of the Royal Academy of Fine Arts in Stockholm.

Photo Credits

Kevin Alter: 28 (bottom right), 32, 40 (bottom right), 42, 43, 45, 46, 47, 48, 51, 52 (top left), 58, 60, 61, 66 (top right)

Sebastian Bianchi: 82 (bottom right), 88, 90, 93, 109, 112, 114, 115

Fernando Maldonado: 117, 118, 119

Patricio Mardones: 89, 94, 95, 96, 101, 106, 108, 110, 111, 113

Cristobal Palma: 14, 24, 25, 26, 27, 28 (top left), 29, 30, 31, 33, 34, 35, 36, 37, 38, 39, 40 (top left) 41, 49, 50, 52 (bottom right), 53, 54, 55, 56, 57, 59, 62, 63, 64, 65, 66 (bottom right), 67, 72, 78, 79, 82 (top left), 83, 85, 87, 91, 97, 98, 100, 102, 103, 104, 105, 107

Project Information and Credits
House at Punta Pite

Architect
Smiljan Radic Clarke

Draft Drawings
Loreto Lyon, Danilo Lazcano

Modeling
Gonzalo Torres

Model Photography
Hugo Lagos

Structural Engineering
Ingenieros Valladares

Technical Inspection
Manual Arriagada

Construction
Constructora Los Alerces Ltda.

Illumination
Interdesign, Eduardo Godoy.

Electrical Installation
Hector Acuña

Heating Installation
Jorge Jaña

Sanitary Installation
Enrique Manrique

Location
Papudo, Fifth Region, Chile

Constructive System
Reinforced concrete

Partitions and Roofs
Glass, reinforced concrete

Interior Terminations
Demolition wood, glass tiles, travertine

Terrain Surface	15,000 m2
Constructed Surface	400 m2
Exterior Surfaces	795 m2
Budget (U$/m2)	950

Project Information and Credits
Crypt in the Cathedral of Santiago de Chilé

Architects
Rodrigo Pérez de Arce
Patricio Mardones
Sebastián Bianchi

Client
Cabildo Metropolitano

Site direction
Dean Damián Acuña

Collaborators
Edmundo Browne, Nicolás Palominos (site and detail design)
Erik Tschaikner, Carolina Portugueis (competition)
Cristobal Dagnino (archeology)

Structural Engineering
Rodríguez & Goldsack engineers

Building Constructor
SALFACORP S.A.

Site direction
Juan Martínez, Gabriel Campos engineers

Heating
Greentek Ltd.

Electrical
MEICSA S.A.

Lighting
Limarí Light Design

Designer in charge
Pascal Chautard

Art pieces conservation and montage
Museo Chileno de Arte Precolombino

Conservator in charge
Andrés Rosales

Art pieces restoration
Ana María Luchinni

Stone restoration and montage
Marta Almarza

Archeology
Ciprés Consultants Ltd

Site direction
Pilar Rivas

Graphic Design
Taller de Ediciones Escuela de Arquitectura y Diseños, Pontificia Universidad Católica de Valparaíso

Designer in charge
Jaime Reyes

Main Altar sculpture
Marcela Correa

Ornamental glass west window
Cecilia Martner

Metropolitan Cathedral Floor Area	7.680 m2
Project Surface Crypt	202 m2
Civic Crypt	21 m2
Presbytery Renovation	378 m2
Apse Renovation	67 m2